DIAMOND MIKE WATSON

# THE LEGEND OF

# *Why Mom Deserves a* Diamond®

ISBN 978-1-891665-48-6

Diamond Mike Watson

Moon Over Mountains Publishing
1528 Brookhollow Drive, Suite 200
Santa Ana, CA 92705 U.S.A.

info@WhyMomDeservesADiamond.com

www.WhyMomDeservesADiamond.com
www.GalleryOfDiamonds.com
www.DiamondWatson.com
www.FlyUpFoundation.com


Cover. Top row: Diamond Mike Watson, Margaret and Ruth Ketchersid.
Second row: Sue and Gina Kim, Gerlyn and Michael Glidden, Jodi and
Tyler Buttle.

Also by Diamond Mike Watson:

Moon Over Mountains - The Search for Mom
Tales of Imagination - Everything is Real
Adopted Like Me – Chosen to Search for Truth, Identity, and a Birthmother
In Search of Mom – Journey of an Adoptee
Why Mom Deserves a Diamond - 1993- Essay Winners
Why Mom Deserves a Diamond - 1994- Essay Winners
Why Mom Deserves a Diamond - 1995- 391 Essay Winners
Why Mom Deserves a Diamond - 1996- 732 Essay Winners
Why Mom Deserves a Diamond - 1997- 1,002 Essay Winners
Why Mom Deserves a Diamond - 1998- 1,500 Essay Winners
Why Mom Deserves a Diamond - 1999- Seventh Anniversary Edition
Why Mom Deserves a Diamond - 2000- A Millennium Mother's Day Tribute
Why Mom Deserves a Diamond - 2001- The Greatest Contest on Earth
Why Mom Deserves a Diamond - 2002- 10th Anniversary
Why Mom Deserves a Diamond - 2003- The Legendary Contest
Why Mom Deserves a Diamond - 2004 - Twelve Years of Love
Why Mom Deserves a Diamond - 2005- Words of Love
Why Mom Deserves a Diamond - 2006- Beyond the Goddess Venus
Why Mom Deserves a Diamond - 2007- Sparkling Treasures
Why Mom Deserves a Diamond - 2008- The Crystal Heart
Why Mom Deserves a Diamond - 2009-The Encouraging Branch
Why Mom Deserves a Diamond - 2010- Discovered With Great Bliss
Why Mom Deserves a Diamond - 2011- Legacy Edition
Why Mom Deserves a Diamond - 2012- A Gift of Love

Dedication

Because She Loved Me First

Martha Velia Watson
March 15, 1920 – September 14, 2006

# Table of Contents


Acknowledgments 7
Foreword - The Man in a Purple Tie 9
Introduction 13


## Part One


In Honor of All Moms 17
History Timeline 31
How Important is a Hug? 35
"I love my mother" 38
Power of Spoken Words 39
The Importance of Handwriting 41
What is the Real Prize? 43
Who Are the Real Winners? 44
The Benefit of Giving 47
The Value of Something Earned 49
The Choice of Words 51
Love is the Answer 54
Top 500 Words 58

# Part Two


Past Diamond Winners  65


# Part Three


The Culture of Why Mom Deserves a Diamond  101
A Timeline in Photos  105
Stepping Beyond Yourself  117
Raise Your Umbrella™  121
FlyUp!™ Fully Live Your Unlimited Potential™  123
The Story of Mother's Day  127

Glossary  129
Bibliography  131
Index  133

# Acknowledgments

Thanks to:

The thousands of teachers who have played such an important part in the contest. Many of you are now old friends. For those I have not had the pleasure of meeting, I feel I know you from the mountains of entries that come across my desk every year with your names written on them. If it were not for you, there would not be this legendary contest.

You may not realize the positive impact you have made in your school, community, and even the world. In addition to fulfilling a writing assignment, you are also allowing your students to ponder and reflect about a person who has a direct influence in their lives.

When you say the contest fulfills the Common Core Standards of figurative language and enhances creative writing skills, this is just the beginning. We may never fully understand the positive impact we are making in the lives of these young adults. When winners come to select their gemstone prizes, they are so proud, which is the first step in building self-esteem.

Win or lose, the beautiful words students write will reach all sentient beings. When a child is chosen for his or her creative efforts it is a wonderful feeling, a great confidence builder, and prepares them for all the success that life is ready to offer.

My Mom, Martha Velia Watson, the only mother I have ever known. Thank you for your courage in allowing me to search for my beginnings. I love you because you first loved me.

My beautiful wife, Maria del Carmen. I remember both the fright and exhilaration as we opened a new business. It has been said that life is about risking everything for a dream that no one can see but yourself. Thank you for staying by my side as we bravely forged ahead, even during times of weariness and doubt. Although we never fully knew our destination, we did know we were traveling in a direction that would one day benefit our world.

My daughters Patricia and Michaela.

My executive assistant, Ra Avis, for her unwavering support, for meticulously checking the word statistics for nearly 100,000 essay winners, and for editing this book. It is not often that an entrepreneur is blessed with one who understands his dreams. Thank you for your dedication, for seeing beyond the fog that sometimes obscured our path, and for joining me to assemble a more loving world.

My extraordinary staff who helped perpetuate the Legendary Contest®. To establish a nationwide tribute of this magnitude has required extreme dedication. You have shared my vision in making it the greatest contest on earth.

The gemstone winners–it has been an honor to meet you and your mothers. Listening to you recite your words of love has made us all better persons.

There are so many people responsible for this book. Forgive me if you do not see your name listed.

# Foreword

In the early morning, on a whim, I responded to the most enthusiastic job ad I'd ever seen.  It proclaimed:

*Job of a Lifetime.*
*Dress sharp, bring four outstanding references*
*and be prepared for us to test your skills.*

I was curious, so I called.

I had a good feeling, even though I had no idea what the job actually entailed.  I had read the websites thoroughly, but none of the puzzling pieces really fit. An author, who was adopted, started a jewelry store that runs a contest for kids?

The day of my interview, the sky was foggy and gray. The jewelry store opened and the Man in a Purple Tie stepped out and held the door for me.  He dramatically took in a deep breath of smog-infested air and proclaimed, "Today is a beautiful day."  I watched his facial expressions for a full minute before realizing that he wasn't joking.  It was an idea he truly believed, and one I heard expressed daily for years.  The oddest thing about it was... he was always right.

The Man in the Purple Tie introduced himself.
He was Diamond Mike Watson.

He pointed out a star– a little light, glowing around the seem-
ingly-solid idea that we make our own reality– and we traveled
there.  We walked from light to light, following freckle and
sparkle, especially those tempered with imperfection.
You can enjoy flaws if you realize every diamond has them.

As The Man in the Purple Tie charged forward fearlessly, I
scrambled behind– still eyeing the blankness of my universe
behind me. What if we fall? I thought, not bothering to speak
the worry into existence, because I knew what he would say:
*What if we fly?*

After three years, I had to quit the company for personal reasons.  Sometimes you have to dive into the blankness to light it
up again.  When I was able to return, I worried I had forgotten
how to be a part of the Why Mom Deserves a Diamond journey.  I worried I had forgotten how to walk on stars.

But on my desk were my keys, exactly as I left them over a
year before. As I rattled them in my hands, I remembered all
the things that are so easy to forget– what faerie dust feels like,
where to find the best stars to dance on, how to dream.

"I am okay, but I don't have a dream anymore," I confessed
to Diamond Mike, during one of our rambling conversations
about the universe, realities, and everything else.

"I will help you find a few," he said confidently, "The only
problem will be finding one big enough."

What if I fall again? I worried as I tentatively put my foot forward, following spark and sparkle.  As The Man in the Purple Tie first promised, a light formed around a solid idea– I found a job of a lifetime, and I stepped into a diamond star.

My journey is lined with stars and imperfections. You can see both, if you look.

You can appreciate a flaw if you realize that all the pressures pressed into you are part of a larger possibility.

You can step fearlessly into the dark
if you remember that you are your own light.

And you can stop worrying about falling,
if you remember you can fly.

So to Diamond Mike and Carmen Watson, their beautiful daughters, and all the brilliant minds and loving families I've been lucky enough to meet through them–

Thank you, for being a light.

Ra Avis,
*Executive Assistant*
*Why Mom Deserves a Diamond, Inc.*

When we know we are loved, we learn to love ourselves.
When we love ourselves, it is easy to love others.
When we love others, the world becomes our beautiful home.

# Introduction

Many years have passed since the first Diamond Winner claimed her diamond prize. Like buried treasure, Margaret Ketchersid's enchanting poem sparkled deep within the mound of essays that were submitted. I'll never forget that beautiful morning on Mother's Day, 1993, when she presented the precious gem to her mother.

Though the contest began as nothing more than a humble tribute to my adoptive mom and the birthmother I was searching for, it soon sprouted wings and evolved into an event in which thousands of kids could become a little closer to their moms.

As a note to anyone who has witnessed an award ceremony, please don't take anything for granted that takes place inside the walls of Gallery of Diamonds jewelers. Everything has a purpose, and has been slowly grown over the past quarter of a century. The contest serves the essential intention of bringing human connection back into our world. With our new age of technological distractions, more and more people communicate electronically. We constantly turn our attention to computers and smart phones. This has diluted interpersonal interactions that have been so instilled into us since the beginning of civilization. The inflection of our voices, the nuances in our eyebrows, and all the micro expressions we use to communicate our thoughts and feelings are becoming lost in texts and screen monitors. There is nothing that replaces face-to-face exchange, hugs, and verbal communication. Since 1993, the Why Mom Deserves a Diamond contest has always promoted these necessary ingredients.

With the help of my staff, my vision is to offer every child a moment to reflect on why their moms are important. If there is a single message to be learned, it is: knowing we are loved defines us. In a time where written and spoken words of kindness seem uncommon, this exercise is beneficial for society. Today, the quest of Why Mom Deserves a Diamond, Inc. has been to alter the course of history by allowing all children to creatively express their feelings about their mothers.

I owe any success from our primary focus: to offer a precious memory that could be given to a mother and her child. In the creation of the contest, selling mother's jewelry was not an intention but a consequence of mothers who wanted to set their winning gems into a tangible keepsake. I am grateful for every mother who sets her winning gemstone.

My previous books narrate the journey to find my birth origins. The success of this journey is not what I found at the end, but the new path that was illuminated. That is why this book is important. No one, including myself, knew that Margaret's essay would be the beginning of the largest mother's appreciation contest in the nation.

I am thankful to be a witness in the real interactions of thousands of kids and their moms. This book is a short history of the contest.  There is no particular order, as many sections come from cherished observations I have archived in my memoirs over the years.  This is my first attempt to capture the essence of the contest in written form.

The contest is in honor of all moms, and all those who are significant in our lives. As the founder who has nurtured it since its birth, I am thrilled to tell the story.

# PART ONE
# In Honor of All Moms

Martha Watson.  Age 86.

I was always curious to know about the woman who gave birth to me. I was adopted at three days old, began the quest for my birthmother at seventeen, and spent nearly twenty years searching for my birth origins. Although my hope diminished in finding my biological beginnings, I wanted to give kids the chance to show their appreciation for their own moms. In 1991, I established a jewelry store called Gallery of Diamonds. The diamond business had been my profession since college, and it was also my talent and passion. As the jewelry store grew, I wanted to do something that would leave a positive impact and create goodwill in the world. I wondered what unforgettable life experience I could offer others.

In 1993 the idea struck to sponsor a writing contest in recognition of my *two* moms– the one who raised me and the one who gave birth to me. I really wanted to know how kids would express themselves for the woman who gave birth to them. What would they say? What words would they use?

I called the principals of a few high schools to invite their students to write a paper on, *Why Mom Deserves a Diamond*. The contestant who penned the most creative essay would receive a quarter-carat diamond to give to his or her mother. During those days there was no entry form, no word limit and no strict rules.

The contest would be in honor of my adoptive mother and the birthmother I was searching for.  It would give kids a chance to recognize their biological mothers, adoptive mothers, and all those who were meaningful in their lives.

During the next few weeks, I received over two hundred entries from students who poured out their hearts, poetically illustrating why their moms should merit the precious gem. At home, I reviewed each labor of love from the comfort of my sofa. After reading each composition, I sorted them into two piles, and continued to evaluate them by grade level, sincerity, and writing talent.

I was engulfed with an indescribable feeling of wholeness. It was fascinating how each student expressed their appreciation for the women who brought them into the world, and I could relate to most of their writings as if they were speaking about my own adoptive mother. I was given a wonderful childhood filled with great memories from a woman who loved me. I had learned from an early age it is the person who gives love, nurture, and caring instruction that is one's true mother. With vibrant imagination, these young adults approached the voluntary writing assignment as a once-in-a-lifetime chance to honor their moms. I was captivated how memories of our mothers brought forth these heartfelt poems, and I realized how our mothers always linger in our consciousness.

While the school system required students to write reports on presidents, explorers, and persons who did not directly impact their lives, the contest offered the opportunity to reflect about a significant person in one's life.

It is ironic that while reading hundreds of these essays, I was also still searching for the woman who gave birth to me. It is even more ironic that one year later I would discover the whereabouts of my birthmother.  Sadly, she had died before I had a chance to meet her. The following years, the Why Mom Deserves a Diamond contest became even more symbolic as an exercise on love, and instilled a moral for all to appreciate one's own parents, whether adoptive or not, and especially while they were *living*.

In a deeper sense, the contest promoted love, appreciation, and offered a prize that never faded– the eternal words of the essay. From the thousands of writings that came years later, the contest helped define the meaning of "mom."  I did not realize the contest would eventually touch the hearts of millions of people.  I would later understand that the burning desire from kids from every age and socioeconomic background was more than winning a gemstone. The stronger purpose was to honor their mothers with words.

After I finished reading the last entry, I realized that a universal element– mom, brought out the most creative expression of love, and that it was a common denominator of everyone's mind and heart. A submission from a sophomore moved me, and I declared Margaret Ketchersid the first grand prize Diamond Winner. I remember how I was mesmerized by her magical words.  To this day, her enchanted essay lives brightly, and continues to have a positive impact in our lives.

Her essay can be read in Part Two, Past Diamond Winners.

On Mother's Day, May 9, 1993, Margaret presented the diamond to her mother, Ruth. My soon-to-be wife, Carmen, took a photo in case the event became legendary. No one knew, including myself, that this fairy tale day would be the beginning of the largest mothers appreciation contest in the nation. A freelance journalist was the only other witness to this special homage, and wrote the following words four years later:

Dorothy Jean, writer.

*"I remember the day in May 1993, when I was interviewing jeweler (Diamond Mike) Watson about his very first Why Mom Deserves a Diamond contest.*

*Just then, a teenager from Edison High School walked into the store with her mother. They came to pick up the first prize - an unmounted quarter-carat diamond the girl had won for her mother by writing the best entry.*

*I don't know who was more excited: the girl, her mother, Michael or I. All I know is that I still feel tingly recalling that moment."*

*Dorothy Jean, May 1, 1997. Jeweler Awards Gem in Why Mom Deserves a Diamond contest. Costa Mesa Breeze.*

I felt it was unfair for only one individual out of two hundred win a prize. I re-read the essays once again and selected fifty second-place winners, choosing to award them red garnets imported from Africa. Although less valuable than the grand prize, they glowed magnificently with a rich, pomegranate color.

On the evening of that same day, I called the second-place winners. Each student had written their telephone numbers on their letters in case they were chosen. I told the mothers who answered that if they brought their child to our jewelry store I would give them a garnet gemstone to commemorate their child's outstanding essay. Most were overjoyed, some were shocked, a few were wary.

Over the next few days, the fledgling jewelry boutique became so crowded that families would sometimes be waiting outside because there was standing room only. Each child and mom would embrace tightly. Many mothers had no idea what their child had written until they came. Using jeweler's tweezers, each child seized their winning garnet from a parcel of gems and placed the stone into their mother's palm.

An anthology of the winning entries were later typed and assembled into a pamphlet entitled, *Why Mom Deserves a Diamond- In Remembrance of Mother's Day - 1993*. Now winners were also published authors.

It is awesome to understand the brief moment I wanted to dedicate in recognizing writing achievement would blossom into so many positive aspects in the lives of a mother and a her child. Writers would be motivated to do their best, gemstone winners would be filled with confidence and self-esteem, and mothers would receive a gem that would endure as a symbol of their child's appreciation.

Looking back, I understand those few families who came with apprehension. Our society has instilled a defense mechanism in each of us to understand that few things in life are free.

I do know the success of the contest came from its sincerity of awarding a prize without expecting anything in return.

In 1994, the fervor of the second contest commenced. That year it was announced that a diamond would be awarded for the grand prize, ten sapphires for first place winners, and two hundred garnets for second place winners. The word limit was set at one hundred.

Entries bombarded the store by the hundreds.  Teachers would hand-deliver heavy manila folders written by their entire English classes, sometimes winking at me and playfully remarking that the best ones were on top.  Faxes spilled onto the floor.  Parents would submit their children's entries or slip them through the mail slot after hours.  Overnight delivery services would rush single essays. The mailman was constantly bewildered, wondering why a jewelry business would suddenly receive daily basket-loads of mail.

By the deadline, the gentle hill of entries on my desk exploded into a mountain of over fourteen hundred submissions. Once again, a single essay moved me, and one grand prize winner was awarded a diamond while two hundred and ten additional kids were awarded other precious gems. Some moms came in blue jeans, others came dressed up, one mom was led into the store blindfolded, and another rolled through the door in a wheelchair. Although the store constantly swarmed with students, I believe I was fortunate enough to meet every family.

The gemstones were the same quality, but I again offered each student the excitement of plucking his or her own colorful prize from the parcel with a pair of jeweler's tweezers.

The sharp and shiny metal device was later replaced by a safer, plastic version. The ritual of choosing a gemstone became a tradition that has endured until today.

The winners would then release the gemstone into their mothers open palm. For the ten sapphire winners, the employees would acknowledge their accomplishment by clapping. Soon the entire store would echo with applause.

We published a second anthology booklet of the 1994 winners and donated the proceeds to the Orange County Public Library system. It was a delightful feeling to send a check for seven hundred dollars. The library system purchased books about creative writing, public expression, and resource books for adoptees, adoptive parents and birthparents. During the twenty years these anthologies were published, nearly $40,000 was donated to the library system.

The 1995 contest garnered two thousand entries. 1996 yielded nearly five thousand. To keep organized, we carefully opened and sorted each package. The three weeks I devoted to reviewing the entries involuntarily exceeded six weeks, and I began to understand the work of a schoolteacher. This was the first year in which a diamond was awarded to two students. Because of the larger pool of talent, selecting a single "best" candidate became increasingly difficult. In a decision that lasted, there are now two Diamond Winners selected annually from Orange County; one from an elementary grade and another from a middle to high school grade.

By 1997, the amount of essays surpassed five thousand. Stacked in a single vertical pile on a desk, they climbed halfway to the ceiling. Anticipating the growing response, the maximum words were reduced, for if they were not I would surely still be perusing them.

Until this time, I read and selected every gemstone winner. I received much joy from reading, but it was somewhat embarrassing that I was the sole judge. As a jewelry store owner, most persons would think my duties would be jewelry-related. I did need help, and it seemed the teachers themselves would be the obvious solution. However, would it be a legitimate contest if a teacher graded his or her own students writing? Someone had to judge the essays. A solution needed to be discovered. The epiphany came a few days later– Teachers would judge the essays with the agreement that the essays did not come from their own school. That way, there was no possibility of bias, for each teacher would have no connection with the authors. The problem was solved and a comprehensive judging manual was written.

In 1998, the contest was expanded outside of Orange County to Los Angeles County. A team of panel judges were chosen. Several thousand more essays were submitted and two additional Diamond Winners were selected.

By 2000, the contest spread to the entire states of New York, Michigan, Texas, Ohio, California, and Indiana. A staggering amount of essays were submitted and eight quarter-carat diamonds were awarded.

# 2001.  An Awakening

We can never be thankful enough for the person that nurtures and instructs us through life. Some persons did not receive the great love I received from my mother.

I am who I am because I know someone loved me.

I like to think that most of us make independent choices. We are not string-guided puppets.  However, the choices we make are many times determined by the morals that are instilled into us as children.  That is why I am sharing the following story.

During the holiday season of 2001, shortly after 9/11, two masked men barged into Gallery of Diamonds aiming guns at my assistant and myself.  While standing behind my desk, a metal barrel was pointed at my chest.  We were ordered onto the floor while the disguised men proceeded to steal the jewelry.

The next brief moments seemed like eternity, and we were certain we would be harmed. Lying face down on the floor, flashes of our lives played in our minds as the robbers ransacked the store.  A holiday bell was attached to the front door and its jingle was the last sound heard as the gunmen fled. As we rose to the eerie silence, many jewelry showcases were empty and in chaos. The gemstones that were to be awarded to winners the following year were stolen.

Luckily, we escaped harm and the insurance company helped refurbish the inventory.

I still remember the gunman's eyes, which glared beneath a black ski mask. Today I wonder what his family life was like and what kind of parents he had. Perhaps the gunman did not feel what he did was wrong, and was taught to get ahead in life one must plunder. And to be extreme, if I had the same parents as the gunman, perhaps I would have *been* the gunman, pointing the weapon at another with my finger on the trigger. Days later, after my fear dwindled, I understood that it would be outside my character to rob another. It would be the *right choice* for me to not rob someone. The gunman, however, may have felt he was making the *right choice.*

Most people seem to embrace an essence, and most of us are who we are the duration of our lives. I believe a large part of our essence is absorbed from others. In my case, I learned the beauty of the universe not from the biological information passed down from my ancestors, but from the only mother I have ever known- my adoptive mother.

Loving and respecting oneself and others must be learned. It must be taught and absorbed. That is one of the reasons I created the Why Mom Deserves a Diamond contest. It is important to experience life's tragedies as awakenings. Sometimes it takes a dramatic event to understand the deeper mysteries of life.

My adoptive mother died in 2006. I was thrilled that she had the chance to fly to California to see the contest in action. She loved kids and watched them run in by the dozens with their mothers. I wonder if she knew she would one day inspire the world's largest mother's contest.

The decision was made to eliminate the out-of-state division of the contest. Ideas ran out on how to allow non-local winners to fully experience the joy of the interpersonal interactions accessible to Orange County families.

On October 10, 2006, Gallery of Diamonds was asked to move, and given 30 days notice. The landlord explained that a larger business wanted its current location and so they would not renew another lease. After sixteen years, Gallery of Diamonds faced the challenge of being without a home for the holidays. A two-week extension was granted, and the company found a location one mile away. In six weeks, the suite was designed, the showcases were installed, and security was obtained. For the first time, the store would have an identity in Newport Beach. Why Mom Deserves a Diamond was established as a corporation.

In 2010, the company became a franchise. It seemed an ingenious idea for expansion, and offered the potential to successfully expand the contest throughout the nation. A confidential operations manual was drafted. The trade secrets were memorized and the book was locked in a safe. I flew to Illinois to draw the contracts. It was only after we officially became a franchisor that I realized the yearly administration costs and responsibilities associated with such a complex entity. We did not become like a McDonald's restaurant, we became like McDonald's *headquarters*.

Also, we were not assured potential franchisees would manage the company with the heart and integrity that was responsible for the contest's creation and success. Although all organizations need to make income, the grand purpose of the contest was to *give* to others, not to take. The grand purpose was to offer an unforgettable human experience to a mother and her child.

Since this book was published, we have halted franchising attempts. We have taken another breath to rethink the most feasible way to spread the contest in a way that ensures the greatest benefit for all.

---

In 2011, to illustrate how a simple idea could touch millions of people, every member of our staff simultaneously launched a biodegradable balloon filled with pink carnation seeds. Every balloon represented the employee's appreciation for his or her mother. The seeds represented how love could grow and unfold from the love we learn from others.

In 2015, the company moved once again to a third, larger location in Santa Ana. It was imperative to find a place that could accommodate thousands of families. It is where our headquarters currently resides and contains a quiet room specifically for dreaming how to spread the contest to the ends of the earth.

# History Timeline of Gallery of Diamonds and the Contest

*1991.*

September 15. Gallery of Diamonds is opened in the city of Costa Mesa, CA.

*1993.*

May 9. First year of contest. 250 essays submitted. First Diamond Winner awarded. July 23, Diamond Mike marries Carmen Ortiz.

*1994.*

September 4. Two families united as one. At age 36, after searching for nearly twenty years, Diamond Mike meets his biological family for the first time at his childhood home in New Albany, Indiana.

*1996.*

Gallery of Diamonds awarded Holiday Spirit of the Year award from the Orange County Register. Begins to award two Diamond Winners annually.

***1997.***

Submissions surpass 5,000. A guidebook is created for contest panel judges.

***1998.***

Contest begins to include other states. Submissions surpass 10,000.

Author's first autobiography, *In Search of Mom* published.

***1999.***

Gold hits a 20-year low of $252 per ounce.

***2000.***

Contest expanded to entire states of California, Texas, Indiana, Pennsylvania, New York, Ohio, and Michigan. Eight diamonds awarded.

***2001.***

Armed robbery of all diamonds and winning gemstones to be awarded following year. All gemstones were replaced.

***2002.***

*Why Mom Deserves a Diamond* trademark granted.

***2003.***

Contest expanded to 48 states. Gallery of Diamonds generates $5,000 in anthology book proceeds for Orange County public library system.

***2004.***

Master database of every winning essay since 1993 created.

***2005.***

March 19. After sending cease and desist letter for infringing, a large American jewelry chain files to cancel Why Mom Deserves a Diamond trademark based on Lanham Act.

**2006.**

September 14. Founder's adoptive mother, Martha Watson, dies at the age of 86.

**2007.**

March 22. United States Patent and Trademark office finds itself in favor of Gallery Of Diamonds trademark and case is dismissed with prejudice.

Company outgrows headquarters and moves to Newport Beach, CA.

In memory of founder's adopted mother, two heart-shaped diamonds are awarded to Diamond Winners.

*The Legendary Contest* trademark granted.

Company introduces *Moon Over Mountains* (M.O.M.) mother's jewelry.

**2008.**

Replaced jewelers metal tweezers used by winners for safer, plastic version.

*Moon Over Mountains* trademark granted.

**2009.**

July 23. Why Mom Deserves a Diamond incorporates.

World gold price begins a steady increase. Sterling silver jewelry introduced.

*Arms of Love®* symbol created.

**2010.**

From March through June, over three thousand families come to Gallery of Diamonds for the Why Mom Deserves a Diamond experience.

The company becomes a fractional franchise.

*2011.*

Gallery of Diamonds celebrates 20-year anniversary.

World price of gold tops historical record of $1900 per ounce.

Company releases balloons filled with pink carnation seeds in honor all moms.

Program named Raise Your Balloon begins.

First diamond is awarded to a first-grader.

*2012.*

Last year annual anthology book published. To conceal identity of minors, names of winners replaced with first name and last initial.

Team films series of employee videos.

Teachers integrate contest into the Common Core State-Standards of figurative language.

*2014.*

Raise Your Umbrella school program begins to promote self-confidence. The black and white umbrella becomes a symbol of pride and self-esteem.

*2015.*

Company outgrows its headquarters once again and relocates to Santa Ana, CA.

Raise Your Umbrella program changes name to FlyUp!.

*2016.*

FlyUp Foundation brings its program to thousands of students in Orange County.

Gallery of Diamonds celebrates 25 years in business.

The 25th contest season is launched.

# How Important is a Hug?

"Give your mom a hug!" has become a commonplace expression that my staff commands to winners. We do this because a shared hug makes the mother and child experience real and unforgettable. For a moment to be remembered, we must use all our human faculties and senses.

I have witnessed the full spectrum of loving interactions from tens of thousands of families who have come to Gallery of Diamonds jewelers for the Why Mom Deserves a Diamond experience. Over the years, I have become an expert in describing the many ways mothers and their kids show affection for each other. My staff and I are professionals in guiding the most memorable experience. We believe it is important in order to ensure every family leaves with a wonderful mother and child memory that will remain with them forever.

I have seen many kids who were reluctant to show their physical affection toward their mothers. Perhaps they wanted to appear cool in front of their peers, or maybe they came from a family that did not show much physical interaction.

Moms also show their love and affection in different ways.

When a child reads their words of appreciation and presents a gemstone prize to his or her mom, there are so many ways a mother will respond.  Some simply say thanks. Some cry with joy.

I enjoy the interactions where a mom embraces her child tightly.  My own adoptive mother was a hugger, and experiencing that helps me recall the warm embrace of my mother. One striking thing is that a mom's reaction will have nothing to do with the content of the words.  It does not make a difference if an essay is eloquent or trite, deep or shallow, long or short, poem or prose.  It also does not make a difference of the monetary value of the prize won.

Kids that are hugged are generally more self-confident and secure. A hug, or simply the gesture of placing a caring arm around another's shoulder is sometimes enough to demonstrate, "Despite any challenges of the world, I love you."

And if it is difficult for one to use physical contact as a

form of human affection, it is important to find other ways to communicate love, such as warm or kind words. This creates a wonderful society of young people who will grow up to accomplish tremendous things.  But of most importance is that kids "know" they are loved.

Knowing we are loved defines us as humans. It creates our true essence. It shapes our view of ourselves and the world around us. You have the power to give this great gift to someone else. Don't pass up an opportunity to hug someone you love.

# I love my mother.

The following expressions say, "I love my mother." Each was written by mothers, fathers and essay winners whose origins trace to the far corners of the world.

**Armenian**

**Ethiopian**

**Hebrew**

**Chinese**

Annemi çok seviyorum
**Turkish**

**Hindi**

**Sign Language**

Tôi yêu mẹ tôi.
**Vietnamese**

Aku sayang Ibu
**Indonesian**

JA VOLIM MOJU MAJKU
**Croatian**

**Lao**

**Japanese**

Я люблю мою маму!
**Russian**

J'aime ma mère
**French**

**Braille**

**Georgian**

Jag älskar min mama.
**Swedish**

T'hibirkem yemma
**Bereber**

Аз обичам моята майка!
**Bulgarian**

**Farsi**

**Cambodian**

**Kannada**

Kocham moją mamę
**Polish**

**Arabic**

**Korean**

Yo quiero a mi mama
**Spanish**

Mahal ko ang inay ko.
**Tagalog**

**Egyptian**

**Tamil**

# Power of Spoken Words

When winners were first asked to read their essays, it became a lesson for all. We discovered the power of the spoken word. Nowadays, as each young author recites their poem aloud, the words seem to emit a sense of hope and comfort. We learned that sincere words that are spoken have the amazing ability to heal, encourage, and inspire. Throughout our lives, we remember beautiful words that are spoken to us.

*When words are written, they become part of our thoughts. When words come forth from the lips, they become real.*

Beautiful words of appreciation must be thought, written, and spoken aloud. They can be one of the greatest gifts. I'm certain every mom and child who has come to Gallery of Diamonds has remembered that magical moment. And, by being recognized, every child receives a sense of pride and fulfillment that endures their entire lives.

Some may think the Why Mom Deserves a Diamond contest is just a simple writing assignment, but over the years it has become a launching pad of self-esteem for thousands of kids who are now adults.

So quick to comfort, so easy to cling to
Her soft soothing words, I yearn for and cherish
Her worn silken hand I always hold tightly,
Her bare little shoulder that absorbed many tears,
A motherly touch that only she can give.
If I could reach the beautiful moon up above
I'd surely give it to her with all my love
In return for those self~made gifts of love
This motherly angel of mine deserves a beautiful diamond.

Your name Dominique Hilsabeck

The timeless words from a seventh-grader in the 1994 contest. "The fluid process of cursive writing demonstrates our intelligence, grace, and creativity."

NY Daily News.

# The Importance of Handwriting

This is how I write my name.

If you never get the chance to meet me, I am glad to share my signature. It contains much of my essence, and if you look closely, much of my personality lives within this signature. You are free to analyze it, and learn about my hopes, dreams, imagination and desires. Surely there is some significance in the forceful pen thrust of the M. And why are the dots of my I's so high? After I leave this world, will the curve of the K or the shape of the final E mean anything? Would you know anything about me if all you saw were the words Diamond Mike typed in a regular font on a piece of paper?

It seems that handwriting is slipping away, and more and more students are using keyboards. Will handwriting become a lost skill or ancient art?

There is much evidence that old-fashioned pen to paper is simply good for our brains, and scientists are discovering that learning cursive is an important tool for cognitive development. Brain imaging studies show that cursive activates more of the brain than keyboarding. In the case of learning cursive writing, the brain integrates sensation, motor control, and thinking.

Although it is true that humans communicate more often on computers and smartphones, I feel we may be losing more than what we are gaining if new school standards eliminate penmanship.

# What is the *Real* Prize?

Since the beginning, I have announced a diamond as the grand prize. From deep within the earth, diamonds are created by the incredible forces of nature. When a diamond is polished, its inner beauty is released, and becomes a prism that can bend white light into every color in the rainbow. Diamonds are the hardest natural substance known. They are rare.

Diamonds are eternal. They are unchanging and beautiful. They are a marvel of nature. They hold our most cherished memories. When given, each glance evokes the memory of the giver. Isn't that also the definition of love? However, that is not the real prize.

The real prize is not the diamond, the gemstones, or any jewelry a mother may set the gemstone into. The real prize is the words a child composes. Sometimes a mother might not comprehend this until the words are spoken from her son or daughter. The winning gemstone serves as a symbol of those words. Although the gemstone has a monetary value, a child's heartfelt expression of love and appreciation is priceless. There is nothing more valuable.

It is imperative for a mother to know the reason she has come to Gallery of Diamonds is to celebrate a moment with her child. However brief, I can attest it is a moment that will be remembered throughout each of their lives.

When a child reads their words of love and selects and places a gemstone into their mothers palm, that gemstone increases in value a million-fold.

The child's words will live in that gemstone forever.

## Who Are the *Real* Winners?

*Children.* Every year, thousands of kids compose words of love for their mothers. They pause, ponder, and reflect on their feelings of appreciation for the woman who gave them life. When winners are announced, they understand that someone took the time to read and evaluate their artistic work. Each winner receives a sense of worth and self-esteem. The pride in being chosen is an unforgettable experience.

*Teachers.* Schoolteachers selected to be contest panel judges invest hundreds of hours evaluating the submissions. It is inevitable that they will be affected by reading these positive words.

*Moms.* Because every gemstone winner is required to recite their words aloud to their moms, these moms feel pride, self-worth, and see a reflection of their kids in themselves. This becomes a wonderful memory that lasts forever.

*The Staff.* When one's job is to award a prize and listen to the words a child has composed for someone significant in their lives, they become energized and fulfilled. It makes them smile and receive a deep understanding of what is important.

*Who benefits?* Everyone the contest touches. It has become a positive force that benefits all of us.

Who are the *real* winners? The entire world.

As the steward and founder, it became my responsibility to lead the contest in a direction that would positively impact millions of people.

# The Benefit of Giving

Can one give too much? Is it possible to go bankrupt from giving? Years ago I remember reading children's books to my youngest daughter. I'm not sure who enjoyed the stories more but there is one tale I will never forget. It was called, *Milo and the Magical Stones*.

Milo was a mouse that lived on an island with other mice. He discovered a beautiful, golden stone in the crevice of the mountain. He saved it and admired its wonderful glow. When other mice discovered his find, they greedily began digging into the mountain, hoarding every shiny stone they found until the mountain collapsed into the sea.

The final pages of the story offered an alternative conclusion: The mountain did not collapse. This happened because the other mice learned from Milo that one should return a treasure back to the island for every treasure it gives. Whenever a mouse retrieved a shiny stone, it would return another stone in its place. The mice spent hours hand-engraving rocks with ornamental designs to show appreciation to their island, then buried it where they found the golden stones. Every mouse had a treasure to enjoy while living on a safe and beautiful island.

A moral of the story is the importance of giving.  It is difficult to enjoy the wonderful fruits of the Earth without sharing one's appreciation.

It may be impossible to give too much. As a side note, I have found that the gift of conversation is sometimes more beneficial to society than a dollar amount one may give.  Sometimes people just want to be acknowledged.  Sometimes they just want someone to communicate with them and listen to them. Whenever I have given, I have never returned to my office broke. I have never been bankrupt.

The act of giving *without expecting anything in return* was the secret of Why Mom Deserves a Diamond's success. The miracle of giving will always return its shiny, golden treasures to the giver.

# The Value of Something Earned

Over the years, I have been misrepresented as a generous jeweler that drops gemstones from the sky for scrambling kids.

The truth is every diamond and gemstone given must be earned. A child must first contemplate and creatively write his

or her appreciation for mom. Next, essays are read and rigor-
ously judged by a qualified teacher that has no connection with
the student.

A child's work does not end there, for if they are selected as
a winner, they are required to come and publicly recite their
words to their mothers.

It is ironic that when Gallery Of Diamonds was established
in 1991, few persons came when a free sapphire was offered
to the first customers who visited the Grand Opening.  A large
newspaper advertisement notified the public that the new
jewelry store would give the genuine blue gemstone to anyone
who simply came.  They did not have to publicly recite anything.  In fact, they didn't even have to write anything.

I learned later that this gift appeared valueless.  Only when
something is earned is it given value.  That is one reason why
every gemstone awarded in the contest is priceless.

# The Choice of Words

In 2006, we began the tedious process of compiling an archive of every winning submission since 1993.

After many years of this work, many people can now come to our headquarters and enjoy our database of these submissions.

Looking deep into this massive archive, it is a remarkable study of how school kids perceive their mothers. Since the prompt and instruction of the assignment, "Why Mom Deserves a Diamond," has remained the same, the archive is a large and rich database of heartfelt love letters about moms written by Orange County kids.

More intense analysis of this data might one day become an important study of psychology and will determine the gradual shift of social values of grade school students. This will be interesting to understand how we have changed as a society.

The 2016 Archive contains 2,382,771 words from 99,560 entries. There are a total of 16,326 unique words.

## Calculating Variables

1.     Future studies will find it interesting to determine how many times a particular word was used by authors during any contest year. However, for accuracy, because the amount of submissions increased over the years, along with the fact that the word limit decreased, it will be necessary to factor that into any calculation.

2.     When given a limitation of one hundred words, for example, a student would have four times the probability of using a particular word than if he or she would be restricted to twenty-five words. Also, even if one is comparing an equal word limitation for any yearly comparison, a particular word may have be used 50% more often simply because 50% more essays were submitted that year. Because of the aforementioned factors, it may be more meaningful to analyze a word or phrase in the context of the "total quantity of words" rather than "total quantity of essays."

3.     Another fact to be taken into consideration are the grade levels contained in the archive. This is important because the vocabulary of a student in a lower grade contains words that are shorter and less complex than a student in a higher grade. In other words, a more complex word that may typically be used by a twelfth grader will show a low frequency rate simply because there are relatively few twelfth graders in the database. The reason for this anomaly is simply because the participation level in the contest is less in higher grades.

Following is the percentage of grade levels contained in the current archive of 99,560 essays.

| Grade | Percent of Archive |
| --- | --- |
| First grade | 3.52% |
| Second grade | 7.32% |
| Third grade | 11.83% |
| Fourth grade | 15.04% |
| Fifth grade | 16.90% |
| Sixth grade | 16.84% |
| Seventh grade | 13.97% |
| Eight grade | 8.09% |
| Ninth grade | 2.57% |
| Tenth grade | 1.43% |
| Eleventh grade | 1.66% |
| Twelfth grade | 0.85% |

4.    *Derivatives and Plurals.* It must be remembered that verbs can be conjugated and nouns have plurals. Therefore, when a verb such as *teach* shows up 88 times, the frequency increases to 1,547 when one adds *teaches*, *teaching* and *taught*. The word *angel* shows up an astonishing 5,816 times. When the plural *angels* is added the frequency jumps to 6,297.

5.    Finally, and most important, it must be clear that the database of essays are the winners chosen. The thousands of essays that were not selected as winners were not entered into the database nor factored into the statistics. If every single essay submitted would be taken into consideration, the statistics would be skewed. Also, since contest panel judges are instructed to select the most creative essays, they would indeed select essays with more intriguing word choices.

# *Love* is the Answer.

Because of the title and prompt of the contest, the most common words are; my, mom, deserves, a, diamond, and because. These words must be excluded from the findings. It is striking how a particular word has been constantly used since 1993. Out of the possible 16,326 unique words, the word *love* (along with its derivatives) occurred 53,236  times from 99,560 entries!

It is sometimes important to combine associated words when analyzing the data. For example, love is used 32,472 times. When derivatives or closely related words are added such as: *loves, lovely, lovingful, loved, lovesome, loving, lovingness, loveness, lovable* and *loveable*, the total frequency jumps to 53,326. Out of the 16,326 unique words, this makes the word *love* or its derivative, the eleventh most used word! (The misspelled *loveable* occurred 335 times. The correct spelling, *lovable*, occurred 321 times!)

Therefore, it is fairly accurate to state that nearly 54% of the authors in the archive used the universal word love or a derivative when describing their relationship with their mothers.

*If there is anything real in this world, I'm convinced it is a universal power called love. Whether it is born from our hearts or from a Master Diamond Cutter, I have seen it cross every border of culture and religion. I have heard thousands of kids from every socio-economic background recite their poetic expressions to their moms.*

*Perhaps the love of parents for their children is one of the strongest human emotions. I am grateful I was first loved by my adoptive parents. Like learning all things from our parents, I learned love. It is easy for me to see love in all things. Like the fundamental forces of nature, love is a power I recognize that holds the universe together in wondrous balance.*

Here are a few often-used words (without any derivatives) and the frequency in which they occur.

Total Winning Essays: 99,560.

| Word | Frequency | % of Winners |
| --- | --- | --- |
| Love | 32,472 | 32.6% |
| Always | 16,226 | 16.3% |
| Heart | 14,364 | 14.4% |
| Beautiful | 12,924 | 12.9% |
| Eyes | 11,877 | 11.9% |

It is fascinating to examine a word by itself, then later in context with the actual essay. For example, the word *cactus* shows up twice in the archive. One essay reads, "My mom's love is like a cactus in a dry desert." The other essays reads, "My mom says loving a teenager is like loving a cactus." *Blond* or *blonde* shows up 101 times– "Her long blonde hair is like a river of love." *Architect* was used nine times, and so eloquently– "Thy sculptor of innocence. She, who architects my very soul," and "Creator of my life, designer of my dreams, architect of my reality, the foundation of my being."

Following is a frequency word chart categorized by subjects.

| Affection | | Insects | |
|---|---|---|---|
| Smile | 7,235 | Butterfly | 1,049 |
| Hug | 3,345 | Bee | 362 |
| Kiss | 2,234 | Firefly | 72 |
| Laugh | 1,666 | Ladybug | 36 |
| Sing | 957 | Dragonfly | 17 |

| Celestial | | Sweets | |
|---|---|---|---|
| Star | 7,706 | Candy | 953 |
| Sun | 6,576 | Chocolate | 766 |
| World | 5,695 | Honey | 758 |
| Sky | 4,532 | Sugar | 503 |
| Moon | 1,643 | Cookies | 372 |
| Universe | 534 | Pie | 238 |
| | | Cake | 190 |

| Plants | | Animals | |
|---|---|---|---|
| Rose | 3,921 | Bird | 778 |
| Flower | 2,844 | Bear | 729 |
| Daisy | 213 | Puppy | 248 |
| Violet | 203 | Lion | 235 |
| Sunflower | 130 | Dove | 88 |

| Anatomy | | Nature | |
| --- | --- | --- | --- |
| Heart | 14,643 | Ocean | 1,275 |
| Eyes | 12,319 | Sunshine | 1,052 |
| Hair | 2,169 | Rainbow | 1,044 |
| Face | 1,630 | Sea | 994 |
| Hand | 1,064 | Earth | 852 |

| Colors | | | |
| --- | --- | --- | --- |
| Gold | 3,166 | Brown | 559 |
| Blue | 1,458 | White | 481 |
| Red | 1,065 | | |

If the top 40 words used in the archive were computed to compose a submission in 22 words, the essay would read something like this:

*Mom deserves a diamond because she loves me. Always sweet and loving. Beautiful heart and eyes. I love her in my life.*

Or,

*My sweet mother has a loving heart. The diamond of my life. She is the best of me. I love her always.*

Following is a list of the top 500 words and their frequency used out of the total 16,326 unique words in the archive. This list does not account for derivatives.

# TOP 500
## Words Sorted by Frequency

| Word | Frequency |
|---|---|
| my | 132,168 |
| she | 119,679 |
| a | 101,926 |
| is | 96,263 |
| mom | 89,429 |
| the | 71,848 |
| and | 71,103 |
| me | 69,707 |
| her | 56,027 |
| diamond | 46,446 |
| I | 45,799 |
| like | 38,356 |
| as | 35,085 |
| love | 32,472 |
| to | 32,429 |
| deserves | 31,176 |
| because | 30,129 |
| of | 27,244 |
| in | 26,815 |
| she's | 22,144 |
| for | 21,112 |
| with | 17,513 |
| always | 16,226 |
| mother | 15,713 |
| heart | 14,364 |
| when | 14,295 |
| you | 13,377 |
| beautiful | 12,924 |
| that | 12,792 |
| so | 11,984 |
| eyes | 11,877 |
| best | 9,580 |
| loves | 9,554 |
| are | 9,359 |
| all | 9,231 |
| loving | 8,335 |
| has | 8,255 |
| life | 7,987 |
| very | 7,617 |
| sweet | 7,463 |
| there | 7,229 |
| be | 7,035 |
| than | 6,989 |
| helps | 6,939 |
| an | 6,827 |
| makes | 6,696 |
| sun | 6,421 |
| moms | 6,313 |
| one | 6,285 |
| caring | 6,284 |
| care | 6,207 |
| kind | 6,133 |
| nice | 6,064 |
| on | 5,985 |
| smile | 5,903 |
| angel | 5,816 |
| world | 5,704 |
| shines | 5,672 |
| day | 5,639 |
| bright | 5,452 |
| I'm | 5,423 |
| up | 5,340 |
| from | 5,329 |
| will | 5,226 |
| never | 5,217 |
| hard | 5,169 |
| it | 5,084 |
| can | 4,951 |
| but | 4,918 |
| takes | 4,837 |
| star | 4,758 |
| light | 4,752 |
| more | 4,718 |
| special | 4,578 |
| much | 4,533 |
| sky | 4,374 |
| night | 4,362 |
| who | 4,256 |
| at | 4,249 |
| every | 4,159 |
| cares | 4,080 |
| works | 3,970 |
| everything | 3,965 |
| diamonds | 3,890 |
| gives | 3,875 |
| have | 3,863 |
| through | 3,846 |
| most | 3,736 |
| person | 3,686 |
| why | 3,663 |
| good | 3,631 |
| us | 3,624 |
| does | 3,569 |
| no | 3,458 |
| think | 3,427 |
| just | 3,356 |
| that's | 3,355 |
| would | 3,334 |
| am | 3,289 |
| family | 3,283 |
| ever | 3,219 |
| shining | 3,207 |
| do | 3,184 |
| also | 3,162 |
| rose | 3,075 |
| sparkle | 3,072 |
| pretty | 3,056 |
| what | 3,036 |
| this | 3,006 |
| stars | 2,969 |
| need | 2,932 |
| warm | 2,880 |
| time | 2,877 |
| not | 2,835 |
| your | 2,831 |
| wonderful | 2,736 |
| great | 2,722 |
| way | 2,669 |
| feel | 2,556 |
| happy | 2,489 |
| know | 2,476 |
| mothers | 2,463 |
| hugs | 2,448 |

| | | | | | |
|---|---|---|---|---|---|
| see | 2,423 | face | 1,671 | woman | 1,242 |
| shine | 2,412 | strong | 1,663 | lights | 1,216 |
| precious | 2,396 | food | 1,649 | over | 1,211 |
| if | 2,389 | soft | 1,638 | ocean | 1,206 |
| homework | 2,365 | other | 1,637 | around | 1,186 |
| gold | 2,350 | want | 1,626 | times | 1,174 |
| really | 2,318 | everyone | 1,621 | keeps | 1,173 |
| make | 2,301 | moon | 1,618 | God | 1,164 |
| even | 2,278 | you're | 1,599 | can't | 1,151 |
| sparkles | 2,272 | perfect | 1,573 | many | 1,149 |
| forever | 2,269 | above | 1,572 | smiles | 1,144 |
| things | 2,218 | kisses | 1,570 | brighter | 1,140 |
| flower | 2,191 | should | 1,570 | kindness | 1,135 |
| about | 2,186 | people | 1,543 | happiness | 1,120 |
| hair | 2,173 | pure | 1,520 | mine | 1,120 |
| without | 2,162 | amazing | 1,495 | they | 1,119 |
| we | 2,156 | words | 1,495 | guides | 1,105 |
| out | 2,142 | better | 1,492 | shiny | 1,105 |
| sparkling | 2,102 | everyday | 1,485 | herself | 1,104 |
| get | 2,101 | blue | 1,460 | working | 1,099 |
| give | 2,073 | mommy | 1,444 | awesome | 1,080 |
| friend | 2,062 | jewel | 1,441 | red | 1,059 |
| beauty | 2,045 | work | 1,439 | sunshine | 1,049 |
| lot | 2,043 | full | 1,438 | morning | 1,045 |
| our | 2,023 | any | 1,414 | gift | 1,037 |
| its | 1,999 | sick | 1,408 | shell | 1,037 |
| help | 1,927 | smart | 1,404 | matter | 1,035 |
| gentle | 1,908 | gave | 1,399 | home | 1,031 |
| down | 1,892 | heaven | 1,396 | whole | 1,019 |
| was | 1,887 | sad | 1,391 | giving | 1,008 |
| by | 1,884 | into | 1,380 | looks | 1,004 |
| how | 1,883 | lovely | 1,380 | still | 1,001 |
| anything | 1,875 | fun | 1,375 | away | 990 |
| could | 1,870 | school | 1,375 | say | 990 |
| only | 1,850 | go | 1,371 | nothing | 987 |
| helpful | 1,845 | right | 1,360 | worth | 975 |
| or | 1,813 | something | 1,333 | brightens | 966 |
| soul | 1,758 | dark | 1,320 | hope | 965 |
| joy | 1,723 | look | 1,291 | whenever | 963 |
| too | 1,708 | big | 1,285 | rainbow | 959 |
| voice | 1,700 | funny | 1,275 | fills | 951 |
| cooks | 1,691 | others | 1,274 | candy | 947 |
| gem | 1,679 | been | 1,269 | filled | 946 |

| | | | | | |
|---|---|---|---|---|---|
| hardworking | 945 | back | 755 | crystal | 632 |
| doesn't | 940 | darkness | 754 | sunlight | 632 |
| inside | 940 | chocolate | 740 | sister | 631 |
| sea | 940 | warms | 740 | live | 629 |
| touch | 928 | moonlight | 735 | path | 629 |
| cleans | 923 | treasure | 733 | kiss | 614 |
| house | 912 | hug | 731 | brother | 612 |
| don't | 909 | valuable | 725 | buys | 612 |
| brings | 908 | wind | 723 | side | 612 |
| made | 904 | children | 720 | well | 611 |
| butterfly | 882 | goes | 719 | glows | 609 |
| puts | 882 | safe | 718 | loved | 609 |
| being | 881 | flawless | 717 | which | 607 |
| rare | 881 | kids | 715 | wouldn't | 605 |
| warmth | 881 | keep | 711 | thoughtful | 604 |
| take | 880 | graceful | 707 | says | 602 |
| priceless | 872 | anyone | 706 | now | 601 |
| roses | 864 | someone | 703 | gorgeous | 600 |
| greatest | 857 | knows | 699 | ruby | 598 |
| thing | 853 | cook | 692 | sure | 596 |
| laugh | 851 | comes | 691 | bed | 594 |
| earth | 846 | glistening | 691 | radiant | 593 |
| hero | 844 | hurt | 689 | describe | 590 |
| golden | 843 | lets | 689 | sent | 587 |
| unique | 841 | each | 688 | though | 584 |
| I'll | 836 | little | 687 | after | 581 |
| generous | 835 | done | 683 | wrong | 581 |
| needs | 831 | them | 683 | fire | 580 |
| twinkle | 830 | bear | 677 | taught | 580 |
| smells | 827 | had | 676 | important | 578 |
| deserve | 821 | teaches | 673 | yet | 573 |
| gets | 809 | water | 672 | before | 571 |
| thank | 808 | flowers | 669 | guiding | 569 |
| two | 785 | bad | 667 | sometimes | 566 |
| guardian | 781 | first | 664 | comfort | 565 |
| helping | 779 | shows | 664 | plays | 564 |
| dove | 773 | show | 660 | come | 562 |
| together | 769 | personality | 659 | here | 562 |
| sunset | 764 | means | 657 | hand | 559 |
| honey | 762 | were | 656 | brown | 557 |
| win | 760 | mind | 644 | comforts | 555 |
| cool | 759 | reason | 639 | hands | 555 |
| protects | 759 | room | 634 | calm | 549 |

| | | | | | |
|---|---|---|---|---|---|
| own | 546 | single | 475 | shimmering | 417 |
| days | 544 | white | 475 | everlasting | 416 |
| strength | 544 | arms | 474 | sings | 415 |
| lots | 539 | sweeter | 472 | cannot | 414 |
| end | 538 | rest | 467 | I'd | 413 |
| universe | 538 | laughter | 465 | clean | 412 |
| tries | 535 | likes | 465 | shooting | 412 |
| dinner | 530 | spring | 464 | compare | 411 |
| supports | 529 | cry | 458 | I've | 411 |
| eye | 528 | let | 458 | garden | 410 |
| dazzling | 526 | support | 458 | may | 410 |
| making | 526 | else | 457 | delicate | 409 |
| clear | 525 | long | 456 | million | 409 |
| bird | 524 | tells | 455 | encourages | 408 |
| truly | 521 | holds | 454 | oh | 408 |
| money | 519 | dad | 452 | stands | 408 |
| clothes | 518 | intelligent | 451 | elegant | 405 |
| guide | 517 | tucks | 449 | sparkly | 405 |
| tears | 514 | going | 447 | tell | 405 |
| glowing | 513 | wings | 446 | wants | 405 |
| brightest | 509 | proud | 445 | magnificent | 404 |
| fall | 507 | problems | 444 | tree | 404 |
| feeds | 506 | cheers | 441 | twinkling | 402 |
| sugar | 506 | understanding | 439 | lost | 398 |
| breeze | 503 | air | 438 | deep | 397 |
| summer | 503 | enough | 438 | role | 397 |
| super | 503 | hearts | 438 | until | 397 |
| river | 501 | inspiration | 436 | wish | 396 |
| find | 500 | model | 436 | helped | 395 |
| three | 492 | places | 435 | years | 395 |
| glow | 491 | such | 434 | everywhere | 393 |
| play | 491 | worker | 434 | watching | 391 |
| queen | 491 | grow | 429 | birth | 388 |
| there's | 491 | tender | 429 | place | 388 |
| brilliant | 488 | ask | 427 | since | 387 |
| cold | 488 | rain | 426 | beyond | 385 |
| teacher | 485 | given | 424 | some | 381 |
| then | 485 | blanket | 423 | | |
| angels | 481 | ways | 423 | | |
| compassion | 481 | ring | 422 | | |
| blooming | 479 | new | 421 | | |
| dreams | 476 | these | 420 | | |
| put | 476 | taking | 419 | | |

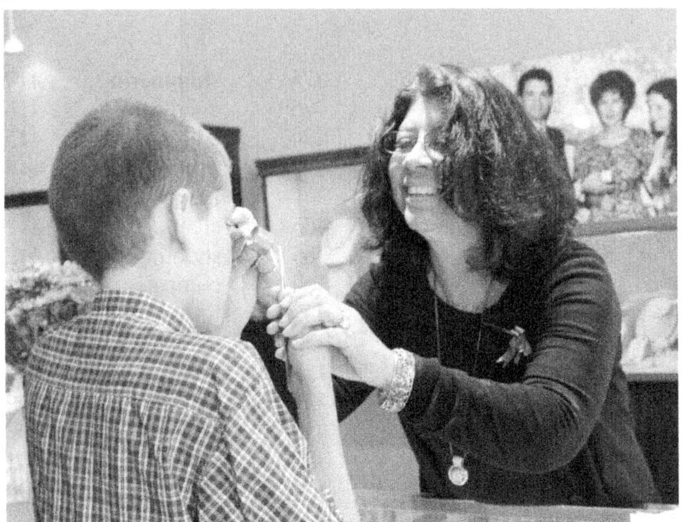

Diamond Day 2013. Carmen Watson shows grade
1-5 category Diamond Winner Tony Scarsciotti
how to examine his winning diamond.

Diamond Day 2013. Gage Butterfield is the Diamond
Winner in the grade 6-12 category.

Diamond Day- 2016. Diamond Day recognizes the achievement of Diamond Winners, and also honors their mothers and every person who is significant in our lives.

# PART TWO
## Diamond Winners

# 1993

Her love is not blind
It is clear and forgiving
Her touch is all-knowing
Her joy is life giving
This angel, my mother, gives of herself
And illuminates me

With compassion's true wealth
A symbol of courage
And strength she remains
And understands all my joys and pains
To gaze at my mother
Who strives beyond duty
Is to see radiate
Her unique warming beauty!

The sweet voice of mother
Her strong, safe, embrace
I long to possess
Her pure, natural, grace
My Mother, my guide
And gemstone so rare
Deserves out of likeness
A diamond as fair

*Margaret Ketchersid, Grade 10*
*Edison High School*
*Huntington Beach, CA*

# 1994

No one knows what it's like
To walk in her shoes
When every game she played with me
She always seemed to lose

And the note from Santa Claus
Seemed to look the same
As the writing on the lunchbags
Where she wrote my name

In all the falls I took
And the cuts I made
She fixed me up with only a
Kiss and a purple band-aid

But of all the things she ever said
And all the nights sleeping in my bed
I promised I'd give her
The diamonds in the sky
When all she said she ever wanted
Were the diamonds in my eyes

*Alison Murphy, Grade 10*
*Capistrano Valley High*
*Mission Viejo, CA*

# 1995

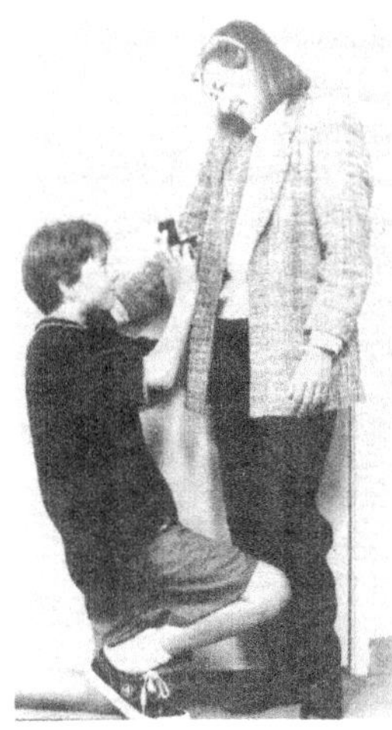

Whether I stand on land or shore
I know I couldn't love my mother more
Always caring, always there
In times that are good
In times of despair
Magical lands we like to explore
When she reads aloud
From classical lore
I thank you, Mom, at each day's end
You really are my best friend

*Scott Kircher, Grade: 6*
*Harbor Day School*
*Corona del Mar, CA*

# 1996

Shadows flickering, dancing about.
Even the moon is terrified.
I lie wide awake, petrified as the distant
Silhouettes come dancing towards me.
Then suddenly they disappear
As she flicks on the light.
Her soothing smile, her comforting voice.
And the monsters are all gone

*Lauren Kiang, Grade 7*
*La Paz Intermediate*
*Mission Viejo, CA*

# 1996

Million gallons of love, two pinches of
creativity, twelve cups of niceness,
two gallons of understanding.
Million drops of unique and
beautifulness, any other items that might
make your mother wonderful.
Mix well, bake two seconds.
I guarantee my mother!

*Megan Darakjian, Grade 4*
*Cordillera Elementary*
*Mission Viejo, CA*

# 1997

Burning sands, ever shifting
Desert of life I must pass through
When I sink, two hands are lifting
Helping me to start anew
She's the oasis where I may rest
She, who always knows me best
Diamond in the rough

*Genevieve Slunka, Grade 11*
*Irvine High School*
*Irvine, CA*

# 1997

My mom is a cozy place
Like a warm cup of cocoa
Or a pillow trimmed with lace
My Mom's love is all mine
I can always depend
She's more than a mom
She's my best friend

*Jessica Barraco, Grade 4*
*Eastshore Elementary*
*Irvine, CA*

# 1998

Her lips are roses,
her complexion is cream.
She understands
my deepest thoughts and dreams.
She is my angel with a halo of gold.
She is my mother.

*Tawyna Ravy, Grade 7*
*Bernardo Yorba Middle*
*Yorba Linda, CA*

# 1998

A heavenly calm,
and pure state of grace.
A lovely expression
falls on her face.
A whisper of words,
like velvety lace.
Soft summer's glow,
in securing embrace.
My Mother.

*Jennifer Plankenhorn, Grade 8*
*Arroyo Seco Junior High*
*Valencia, CA*

# 1998

My mother deserves a diamond
because she's unique, priceless,
perfect, pure, precious, dazzling,
flawless and rare.
She sparkles with love and glistens
with knowledge.
She is a gem to me.

*Vicki Ann Blood, Grade 4*
*St. Pancratius*
*Lakewood, CA*

# 1998

A diamond has all the colors
of the rainbow.
My mom deserves a diamond
because she is all the colors
in my life.

*Jason Kirstein, Grade 3*
*Westwood Basics Plus*
*Irvine, CA*

# 1999

The salt of my life is my mom,
which gives taste
in all the recipes of life.
She is the ingredient
that gives inspiration
in my journey to my goals.

*Roberto Ruiz, Grade 5*
*St. Malachy*
*Los Angeles, CA*

# 1999

Gem of my heart, fair as can be.
A star from heaven brought to earth.
A precious jewel beyond compare.
Deserving this diamond is my angel,
my mother.

*Chris Olsen-Phillips, Grade 6*
*Binford Elementary*
*Bloomington, IN*

# 1999

My mother has a heart of gold.
Her love is the most precious
thing I hold.
And when I look at her I see
An angel sent to protect me.

*Brice Tomlinson, Grade 6*
*Trinity Christian Academy*
*Addison, TX*

# 1999

A rose, pure and true.
Movements of a rainbow.
Voice like silk,
and laughter like the drumming of
raindrops.
Diamond of life.
Sparkling and glittering
with unimaginable beauty.
My mother.

*Paula Kim, Grade 7*
*Los Alisos Intermediate*
*Mission Viejo, CA*

# 1999

Her touch- like breezes on a warm
summer day.  Her laugh- like one million
tears being dried away.  Mom is her name
for which there is no other.  Mom- mine
forever.

*Blair Perkins, Grade 5*
*Taft Elementary*
*Orange, CA*

# 2000

The soothing sound of her voice melts away my sorrow. The gentleness of her touch relieves my deepest pains. The warmth of her sparkling eyes penetrates my soul. Mom.

*Rachel Tomberlin, Grade 7*
*St. Timothy Episcopal*
*Apple Valley, CA*

# 2000

Her hair like the swaying sea
cradling a sunset.
Eyes like two blue sparkling sapphires.
Hands as smooth as gold silk.
A voice soft like the gentle wind.
Mom.

*Sandy Enriquez, Grade 5*
*Gilbert Elementary*
*Garden Grove, CA*

**2000**

A glorious angel sent from heaven, with beauty like a dove. Her voice drains all sadness. A brilliant star shining through the darkness. My friend, my mom.

*Jennifer Scruggs, Grade 5*
*Sleepy Hollow Elementary*
*Amarillo, TX*

**2000**

A flower that blossoms everyday
A stream that always flows
An adventure that has just begun
A book that never ends
A candle that will never die- Mother.

*Tiffany Lamanski, Grade 7*
*St. Pius V*
*Buena Park, CA*

# 2000

A vast lake sparkling with sunlight. A pure meadow with the gentlest breeze. My mother is more beautiful than all of these. My angel. My mother.

*Victor Taylor, Grade 5*
*St. Mary*
*New Albany, IN*

# 2000

My mother's love is like a blanket, shielding me from cold winds of harm. Embraced within her soft touch, I am safe. Sacrificing all, she comforts me forever.

*Laura Cataldi, Grade 10*
*Nardin Academy*
*Buffalo, NY*

**2000**

My mother is an angel. This is true, I know. She's an everlasting hug, that'll never let me go. Knowing that I'm loved, because she told me so.

*Ashley Goodell, Grade 8*
*Chippewa Middle School*
*Okemos, MI*

**2000**

She is like a wave. As tribulations appear in my life, the tide rises and she flows to my side. Her flowing nature calms my storm. Mom, my refuge.

*Ashley Kreidler, Grade 11*
*St. Johns*
*Delphos, OH*

# 2001

Mom is a masterpiece created with love.  Her sparkling smile shines from above.  Bountiful in kindness she proceeds with great care. Without knowing how much I appreciate her there.

*Alyssa Connella, Grade 7*
*La Paz Intermediate*
*Mission Viejo, CA*

# 2001

Behold the ark that bears the covenant of conception. From her womb the living bond arose. And so it is I must behold, my mother, the temple of creation.

*Jesus Hernandez, Jr., Grade 12*
*St. Thomas High School*
*Houston, TX*

# 2001

A beautiful rose that blooms in July.
With bright golden sapphires - those are her eyes.
Her hair is black, like the calm, silent night.
That's my mom alright!

*E.J. Debowski, Grade 4*
*John Malcolm Elementary*
*Laguna Niguel, CA*

# 2002

My beautiful rose is fresh from the garden. Her eyes sparkle like the dew on the soft petals.
Her smile glistens like a rainbow.
She is my charming mother.

*Harry Hudson, Grade 2*
*Bathgate Elementary*
*Mission Viejo, CA*

# 2002

She is a saint,
whose love is great
Giving of herself,
she knows not hate
Kind her eyes,
and soft her touch
Because of her,
I have so much.

*Matthew Scott, Grade 11*
*Heartland High School*
*Belton, MO*

# 2002

My mother is a river meandering
in and out, flowing into every part
of my life. Her banks overflow
with love, kindness, gentleness and
patience.

*Amanda Wheeler, Grade 7*
*Los Alisos Intermediate*
*Mission Viejo, CA*

# 2003

Essence of happiness in this gray world.
She taught me to respect life,
while leaving my footprint.
But in comparison,
mine are as oarstrokes upon the water.

*Logan Cluttey, Grade 8*
*Las Flores Intermediate*
*Rancho Santa Margarita, CA*

# 2003

My mother - a rock, silent and firm.
My mother - a river, peaceful and calm.
Mother - the Sun, warm and loving.
She is the greatest wonder of creation.

*Travis Dziad, Grade 6*
*St. Mary's*
*Greenville, SC*

# 2003

My Mom is like jewels
glimmering through the night sky.
Her eyes sparkle like rain dropping
from the clouds.
I love you mom, all the time.

*Aris Simsarian, Grade 2*
*De Portola Elementary*
*Mission Viejo, CA*

# 2004

Her voice- a chorus of angels.
Her kisses- a butterfly's whisper.
Her spirit-
a gentle summer breeze.

Her love- a deep sea.
My mother…
a precious diamond.

*Tyler Buttle, Grade 5*
*Reilly Elementary*
*Mission Viejo, CA*

# 2004

Eyes sparkling, like iridescent
drops of rain.  Smiles warm,
as hot cocoa on frigid rosebud
lips. Loving, deeper than all the
oceans and seas.  Mother…my
sanctuary.

*Lindsey Croft, Grade 12*
*Nevada Union High*
*Grass Valley, CA*

# 2004

My mother's blue eyes
are magical fountains in heaven.
Her voice calls
upon the angels to sing.
The sunset is a sign
that she is in my heart.

*Erica Haggerty, Grade 8*
*St. Angela Merici*
*Brea, CA*

# 2005

You're spring's showering rain of care. You're summer's shining smile. You're autumn's sweater of warm comfort. You're winter's beauty. You're mother, the seasons of love.

*Jason Punzalan, Grade 9*
*Servite High School*
*Anaheim, CA*

# 2005

Her voice, a nightingale
Her touch, butterfly wings
Her heart, overflowing with love
Her kisses, flawless bubbles
Mom, a perfect gem...a gift forever

*Emily Magers, Grade 6*
*Timberview Middle School*
*Colorado Springs, CO*

# 2005

My mother's eyes are like two fireflies glistening in the moonlit sky.  Her kiss is like a big blue wish.  Mother is nature's way of saying, "Hooray!"

*Analyse Groton, Grade 4*
*Linda Vista Elementary*
*Orange, CA*

# 2006

The definition of love will show her face and speak of endless giving and grace. You'll ask me who this woman is, she's my flawless mother!

*Kevin Banifatemi, Grade 5*
*De Portola Elementary*
*Mission Viejo, CA*

# 2006

Eyes that shine like brilliant stars.
Smile that glows like that of Mars.
Beauty beyond the goddess Venus.
Perfect, my mother, like earth
beneath us.

*Laura Chae, Grade 7*
*Sierra Vista Middle School*
*Irvine, CA*

# 2006

Feeling of safety in her palm.
A touch of warmth in her heart.
Endless love in her eyes.
All points to mom,
my pure guiding light.

*Sera Choi, Grade 7*
*Becker Middle School*
*Las Vegas, NV*

# 2007

Sparkling gold treasures,
snow white doves.
That's mom,
shining beyond and above.
Clear as a raindrop, plain to see.
Mom deserves this diamond,
it's destiny.

*Grace Penner, Grade 5*
*Brookhaven Elementary*
*Placentia, CA*

# 2007

She gave my breath its heat.
She gave my heart its beat.
She allowed love and life to meet.
Without my mom, I am incomplete.

*Michael Glidden, Grade 11*
*Capistrano Valley High*
*Mission Viejo, CA*

## 2008

A little bit of moonlight, a dab of sun.
Then the crystal heart will be yours.
The twinkling light shines like mom's
wonderful eyes.

*Sophia Vazquez, Grade 2*
*Jim Thorpe Fundamental*
*Santa Ana, CA*

## 2008

Her eyes gaze into my soul.
Her heart forged completely of gold.
Her voice melts into crystals of
compassion.
My mother…the gem of me.

*Linda Huynh, Grade 7*
*Fred Moiola*
*Fountain Valley, CA*

# 2009

Eyes glittering with flawless light.
Face perfect as an angel.
She guides me in wisdom.
She is my encouraging branch.
She's my gem of life.

*David Duplissey, Grade 4*
*Ambuehl Elementary*
*San Juan Capistrano, CA*

# 2009

My mother loves as passionately as
a fire in the forge, melting the iron
surrounding our hearts, filling us
with golden compassion and silver
kindness.

*Cheryl Bond, Grade 6*
*Oak Middle School*
*Los Alamitos, CA*

## 2010

My mom is the light in the darkness. She has a heart that is a pure diamond. Her smile gives me loyalty, strength, and courage.

*Harvey Zhou, Grade 4*
*Canyon View Elementary*
*Irvine, CA*

## 2010

Mom, hidden in the earth's soil
Mined, discovered with great bliss
Cleansed, made absolutely perfect
Revealed with brilliant purity

*Thomas Loi, Grade 8*
*Bethel Baptist School*
*Los Alamitos, CA*

# 2011

My mom sings songs to me.
Her songs are as sweet
as hummingbirds.
She fills my heart with caramel.

*Leah Korenberg, Grade 1*
*Los Coyotes Elementary*
*La Palma, CA*

# 2011

Flawless, shining
brilliance of her eyes,
Tender, nurturing
touch of her heart,
Infinite, compelling
wisdom of her words,
My mom:
such a precious jewel.

*Charlie Xu, Grade 8*
*Rancho San Joaquin Middle*
*Irvine, CA*

# 2012

My mom is my balloon.
She lifts me up high
and through the sunset.
She guides me gently
with her string.

*Makenzie Kaufman, Grade 4*
*Vista Verde*
*Irvine, CA*

# 2012

Blossoms envy her lovely face,
with features delicate as lace,
stars imitate her radiant eyes,
but nothing matches her heart in size.

*Lauren Lee, Grade 8*
*Fairmont Private School*
*Santa Ana, CA*

## 2013

Mom is as beautiful
as majestic unicorns
flying into a cloud.
She plays music so beautifully
it sounds like magic
fading away.

*Tony Scarsciotti, Grade 4*
*Benson Elementary*
*Tustin, CA*

## 2013

Stars and galaxies in her eyes,
more beautiful than the finest butterflies.
Mom is beauty and grace
all put into one face.

*Gage Butterfield, Grade 6*
*Crescent Intermediate*
*Anaheim, CA*

# 2014

She's my night's sweet dreams.
My angel in the moonlight watching me.
My mom is the stars
brightening the world.

*Benjamin Pham, Grade 3*
*Courreges Elementary*
*Fountain Valley, CA*

# 2014

An artist,
my mom has created my character,
painted my personality.
Colored by her values,
I am proudly adorned
with her signature.

*Sarah Stern, Grade 11*
*University High*
*Irvine, CA*

# 2014

Seamless ebony cascades.
Fragrant lavender of
warmth and loving care.
Flaming phoenix of ferocity.
Luminous exuberance.
My goddess, my mother,
my diamond.

*Nikki Young, Grade 7*
*MacArthur Fundamental,*
*Santa Ana, CA*

# 2015

The warm hearth that has blazed me
into myself,
has brightened the way through
darkness.
My mom glows with diamond-like
radiance.

*Neha Abbas, Grade 5*
*John O. Tynes*
*Placentia, CA*

# 2015

Thy sculptor of innocence.
She, who architects my very soul.
Playwright of my world.
Purest diamond. Divine author.
I owe her everything.

*Gavin Mosher, Grade 7*
*California Virtual Academy*
*Trabuco Canyon, CA*

# 2016

The sunshine on my playground.
The wind that cradles me.
The light in the darkest cave.
The elements of my life.

*Gina Kim, Grade 5*
*Margaret Landell Elementary*
*Cypress, CA*

# 2016

Rough and blistered hands,
holding me safe.
My light from darkness,
my sanity from madness,
whispering comfort in my ears.

*Danali Olivares, Grade 7*
*Mendez Fundamental*
*Santa Ana, CA*

Today, thousands of people come to Gallery of Diamonds jewelers every year to celebrate a mother and child experience. Many times kids and their families will patiently line up, braced for an experience that will last the remainder of their lives.

During moments of disbelief, I snapped a few photos to freeze those moments in which our jewelry store had transformed into a public podium. I occasionally browse these to assure myself it was not a dream.

The contest is never over, however, for it will now be the beginning of the next. Out of twelve months, the contest takes eight months of preparation. Ideas that were once simple have now become complicated algorithms to choreograph the crowd of excited kids and their moms. I hope this year many more kids will pen their words of appreciation for the person that guides their footsteps through life.

The contest is still in its infancy, and has uncharted continents to explore. I can't help feeling excited about the dreams that are unfolding at this moment; a child's poem is being shown to a neighbor; a child is writing a book that will benefit our world; a child is being reassured that all things are possible.

# PART THREE
## The Culture and Programs of Why Mom Deserves a Diamond

The staff of headquarters narrows down the finest essays submitted to find the next Diamond Winner.

A viral video from a Washington music festival in 2009 showed a shirtless man dancing amongst a crowd of festivalgoers lounging on the grass. The man looked like a maniac even when a second dancer joined him. The first man even seemed to give the other pointers on how to dance. Later, a third and fourth person joined the duet. In less than a minute, hundreds of people were dancing, filling the frame of the anonymous videographer. Before another minute passed, more people were dancing than sitting. A person still sitting would have seemed awkward and out of place.

A movement had sprung.

No organization can exist with a single person or single idea. It requires a team of people who work toward a common goal. It also requires at least another person to follow the "crazy" ideas of the idea-maker. In my case, that was my wife, Carmen, who always seemed to make me look good when others rolled their eyes. Friends cautioned legal troubles. Attorneys warned against lawsuits. I was the shirtless dancer. During the months that followed, more people followed our whim to honor all moms in a national mothers writing contest.

I am so glad I did not hire employees similar to myself, and gambled it would require multi-talents for a company to grow. Although one must be a steward of a company to ensure a positive direction, it is equally important to release the reigns of control and let the genius of one's employees shine. One must hold the vision, yet others must understand and share the vision.

The faithful cooperation from every employee who has worked for Gallery of Diamonds and the Why Mom Deserves a Diamond contest has been responsible for the unbelievable growth and success of each company.

To keep up with the modern world, an organization needs many skills. We have employed software programmers, website masters, jewelry designers, and social media experts. In the early days, some employees actually built the jewelry showcases with wood and screws. They painted the walls. They moved the furniture. No matter one's skill level, or the impressiveness of a resume, however, it has always been a requirement to sustain a positive attitude, a good heart, and the shared desire to leave the world in a better condition than one found it.

# A Timeline in Photos

October 15, the author and his fiancé, Carmen Ortiz, open Gallery of Diamonds jewelers in Costa Mesa, California.

**1993**

July 23, 1993. Author and Carmen Ortiz marry in Laguna
Beach, California.

**1996**

Annual submissions reach 5,000, and approach nearly
25,000 in subsequent years.

1996

Author's adoptive mother, Martha, on left, proudly attends the third annual Diamond Day ceremony.

1998

The Diamond Day award ceremony becomes a magical moment for families to understand the importance of our mothers.

**1998**

Contest spreads to Los Angeles County and four students are declared Diamond Winners.

Carmen Watson selects gemstones to award winners.

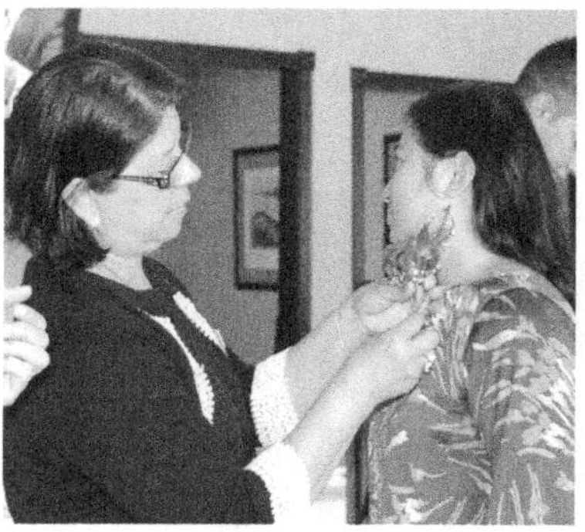

A Diamond Mom has always received a red rose to wear on Diamond Day.

2010

Company first uses the black and white umbrella to symbolize love, self-esteem, and success.

**2011**

To symbolize how words of love can spread across the world, the team of Gallery of Diamonds jewelers launches red balloons filled with pink carnation seeds.

Leah Korenberg becomes the first student in Grade 1 to be honored as a Diamond Winner.

**2011**

Gallery of Diamonds jewelers celebrates its 20th anniversary with purple cake pops and champagne.

With a wagon and boxes, the company attempts to demonstrate the magnitude of participation every year.

**2013**

Northcutt Elementary. Fountain Valley. FlyUp Foundation established to prepare students for a lifetime of success by harnessing the power of positive thinking and expressing appreciation for those who love us.

Dozens of teachers selected as contest panel judges evaluate thousands of submissions every year.

Diamond Day and the gemstone award ceremony has become an unforgettable experience for thousands of families.

2014

Carrillo Elementary. Westminster.
Teachers are shown how to FlyUp!

**2015**

The act of publicly reading one's words of appreciation and giving a gemstone to mom has become a twenty-five year tradition.

To prepare for future growth, Gallery of Diamonds makes its third move to a larger building in Santa Ana.

**2016**

As of this publication, Gallery of Diamonds jeweler's
in Santa Ana, California, provides a home
for tens of thousands of families to experience
the unforgettable power of love and appreciation
between a mother and her child.

It is a tremendous responsibility to be a parent or a teacher. Whether or not we realize it, our kids are watching and listening to everything we do. They are learning and putting all the pieces together.  We are shaping their destinies.  It is important to live our lives the way we would like our kids to live.

# Stepping Beyond Yourself

"Be yourself" is one of the most used phrases of advice in modern history. I remember when my adoptive mother lovingly spoke those same words of encouragement to me. Be yourself shows up in literature, poems, and popular song lyrics. It is the first step in accepting ones passions, dreams, strengths, and shortcomings. To be oneself is to be in one's normal condition or state of mind. It is being satisfied living inside the box in which one is contained. Being oneself is how many of us live because it is comfortable and authentic.

*"Today you are You, that is truer than true.*
*There is no one alive who is Youer than You."*
*- Dr. Seuss*

Stepping beyond oneself, on the other hand, is moving in a positive direction *outside the borders of one's current condition*. It is being "more" of oneself. It is voyaging beyond our imaginary borders that changes the world.

To clarify, being yourself is certainly a better condition than being someone else. We are more fulfilled when we follow our passions rather than trying to meet the expectations of others.

When I say, "stepping beyond yourself," I simply mean being more of who you already are.

Three examples how I stepped beyond myself:

I refused to accept my closed records of adoption. Instead, at seventeen, I began a journey to uncover what became a life-long voyage. My first solo journey by car would be to the Indianapolis courthouse. Twenty years later, I found by biological family. I continue to be an advocate for adoption reform in the release of concealed records.

I captured the attention of a beautiful Guatemalan girl that almost escaped me on the sidewalk the day I arrived in California. I noticed her smile and long, dark hair as I was hauling my belongings into my new dwelling. I married her, and this incredible woman remains my lifelong companion and best friend.

I declined the warning of attorneys to integrate a writing contest into the national school system. Today, Gallery of Diamonds jewelers has become the home of thousands of families, who come every year to celebrate a mother and child experience. It is now in the curriculum of hundreds of schools and is recognized as an institution to promote self-esteem for all kids.

Towards the end of the twentieth century, the expression, "think outside the box" became popular. It became the catchy verbal solution of a nine-dot problem that appeared in Sam Loyd's 1914 Cyclopedia of Puzzles. The problem was to connect all the dots by drawing four straight lines without lifting the pen from the paper.

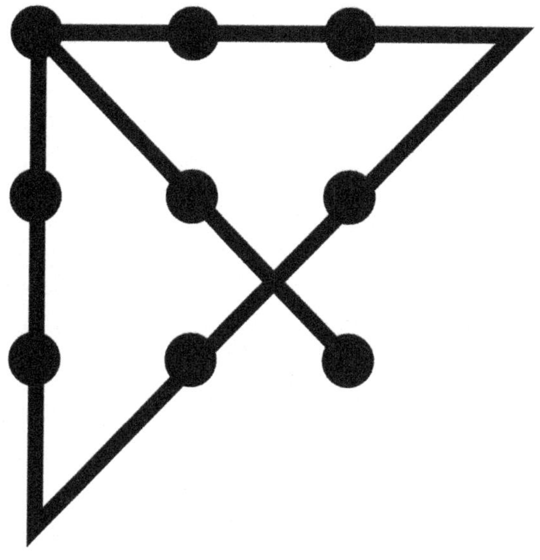

The expression inspired many to understand that one must sometimes look beyond perceived boundaries. Stepping beyond oneself is the courageous leap we must take if we want to see change.

It is alright to find comfort in being oneself. In fact, one must first acknowledge the nine-dot box in which they reside before they are able to step beyond it. Yet, when one takes even a single step beyond the box, the ripple effect can change the universe.

Gage Butterfield, Diamond Winner.

# Raise Your Umbrella™

As we discovered the effects of increasing a child's confidence and self-esteem, the raising of the black and white umbrella became a symbol of this discovery. Our company had to define what it meant to *raise your umbrella.*

As we brought this program into the school system, we realized that sometimes one must be dramatic to prove a point. Today, miniature umbrellas are brought for students to feel the power of stepping beyond themselves into a world of confidence and pride. As each student lifts the canopy above their head, they realize they can become anything they want in life. Throughout our lives, we are constantly reminded of all the things we *cannot* do.  When we are aware of this, it becomes easier to conquer our doubt. As an exhilarating consequence, when we believe in ourselves, our mind makes sure that what we believe is true.

As the umbrellas are passed from student to student, they are asked to raise them above their heads and feel the power of a newfound self-assurance. Some may jokingly shout, "I feel the power!" As they return the umbrellas, I confess that the umbrellas are not magical at all. Then I ask the group from where this power came.  The answer, of course, is from a deep-seated spark that is contained in each of us. In my case, that spark was ignited from the love and encouragement of my adoptive mother. It was not her precise words or even the fact if she actually believed them, but it was more important that *I* believed them.

Since the concepts of FlyUp! And Raise Your Umbrella are similar, they have been integrated together into the same program.  One cannot FlyUp! without first taking the initiative to Raise Your Umbrella. Similarly, when one completes all the steps required in Raise Your Umbrella, then one can FlyUp!

To *Raise Your Umbrella*, you must practice the following:

Step beyond yourself.
Understand that life will give you anything you ask.
Be prepared for everything that life is ready to give you.
Be prepared for a lifetime of success.
Follow your spark, passion, dreams and desires.
Ask with confidence and belief.
Do your best.

# FlyUp!™
# Fully Live Your Unlimited Potential™

Many things excite me. One day I became fixated on the word combination of "unlimited potential." It was such a positive expression, and seemed to summarize my belief in the awesome capabilities of humans. I then realized that it made a positive acronym- "Up!" As I worked with my new word, I wanted to personalize it and later added the word "your" for "Your Unlimited Potential." However, the word "Yup" was comical and did not give justice to the three word combination.

After brainstorming for a better word or phrase, the words "Fly Up" appeared. This uplifting expression demanded beautiful words to define it. Now it was up to the imagination to discover two more words for the letters F and L. I asked friends for advice and received a wild mixture of words and phrases. When "Fully Live Your Unlimited Potential" was discovered, it deserved a logo that would represent its glory. I have sometimes interchanged "Fully" with "Fearlessly", which more specifically addresses the single emotion of fear that stifles the sleeping greatness in each of us.

The invention of FlyUp! came shortly after we created the Raise Your Umbrella school program. The all-inclusiveness of FlyUp! created an even higher form of Raise Your Umbrella.

Many people have heard of Abraham Maslow, who published his 1943 article entitled, *A Theory of Human Motivation*. The paper included a theoretical hierarchy of five levels of human needs.  He found that humans have basic needs such as food, shelter, belonging, and safety.  Higher level needs would include those such as the sense of belonging and relationships. Maslow's theory was that one would not be motivated to obtain a higher level need until a lower level need was satisfied. For example, a person would not desire to earn a college degree before more basics needs such as sleep, air, and shelter were met.

Many people are happy and content at Maslow's third level, which includes loving and being loved, and giving and receiv-

Wilson Elementary. Santa Ana. FlyUp presentation day.

MacArthur Fundamental. Santa Ana.
The author speaks to a class on Career Day.

ing affection. Since not everyone aspires higher levels, the intention of Why Mom Deserves a Diamond is for everyone to cherish this level of happiness.

It is remarkable, however, to see thousands of contest participants boosted to the fourth level, which includes confidence, self-esteem, and achievement. What happens, may I ask, when kids are self-assured, believe they are valuable, and realize they can accomplish anything in life?  Would you agree that is a necessary ingredient for our modern world?

FlyUp! explores the fifth and highest level of Maslow's hierarchy, which is Self Actualization. To Maslow, self-actualization was a state in which one realizes the highest pinnacle of human achievement. This is the most fascinating level. It means self-fulfillment, life knows no boundaries, and understanding all possibilities exist. It is being all one can be. It also shares the idea that we each can *achieve* anything we want from life after we first *define* what we want.

As one accomplishes even one of the requirements for Raise Your Umbrella, that person begins to reach the highest rung of the ladder. Then you fly.

The contest has been a learning experience on life and love for almost every person who has worked for me. While developing a program to motivate my own employees to strive for personal excellence, an expanded program emerged to heighten the experience for every family who came for the contest. My goal was to ensure that each family would leave with a positive memory that would remain with them the rest of their lives. Although our perceptions of life are created from deep within, I felt it was our responsibility to trigger the positive spark that is hidden in all of us.  Even today, our staff focuses their attention on each individual family. It is a brief moment in time, but each family becomes contained in a personal bubble of awareness. They understand the reasons they are there:

- for the child to be recognized for his or her achievement,
- for the family to understand more fully that the greatest gift is a wonderful memory, and
- to celebrate the eternal bond of a mother and her child.

*FlyUp!* is a fresh look at the power of positive thinking and remains an inspirational life and motivational program taught in schools on College and Career Day, at Gallery of Diamonds jewelers, and Why Mom Deserves a Diamond, Inc.

What happens when you Fully Live Your Unlimited Potential?
   You FlyUp!

# The Story of Mother's Day

In 1914, President Woodrow Wilson announced that the second Sunday in May would be the holiday we now call Mother's Day. Although our mothers have been celebrated in many ancient cultures, they have only been nationally recognized for one hundred years.

The hero of this American story is Anna Marie Jarvis, the Mother of Mother's Day.

Anna Marie was born in the tiny town of Webster, West Virginia in 1864. She spent her childhood living in Grafton, West Virginia. Her mother was Anna Reeves Jarvis. She always remembered her own mother's dream of establishing a day to honor all mothers. When Anna Reeves died in 1905, Anna Marie began a mission to create a day in which we could honor the woman who brings us into the world.

Anna Marie Jarvis
May 1, 1864 – Nov 24, 1948

In 1907 Anna Marie gave a white carnation to each mother

in the congregation of her mother's church at St. Andrew's Methodist in Grafton, West Virginia. On May 10, 1908, she held a memorial service in honor of her mother at the church. The bell rang seventy-two times for each year of her mother's life. Anna Marie also wanted children to spend time writing a note of appreciation to their mothers, and during the following years, she began a quest that would change the way we now celebrate this day.  After much public speaking and mailing hundreds of letters to people of power, Anna finally established what we call Mother's Day.

In the early 1920s, "greeting card" companies began selling Mother's Day cards. Jarvis detested this because her intention was for children to compose words from their hearts. Florists marketed carnations, which infuriated Anna Marie so much that she was once arrested for protesting at a Mother's Day carnation sale.  It is ironic to note that although Anna Marie worked almost a decade trying to establish the holiday, she spent the rest of her life trying to end Mother's Day, and invested her family's inheritance campaigning against what the holiday had become. Her intention was reform, not revenue. Her New York Times obituary said she became embittered because too many people sent their mothers a printed greeting card. She said,

*"A printed card means nothing except that you are too lazy to write to the woman who has done more for you than anyone in the world." -Anna Jarvis.*

# Glossary

Arms of Love®: A trademark symbolizing the outstretched arms of a mother holding her child. The mark consists of a vertically elongated backward letter "S," 1/3rd of the way down from the top, with a smaller upward arch protruding to the left. The figure points to the negative integers of time, reminding us of our birth origins. Today, many mother's jewelry designs offered in the contest are etched with this symbol.

Contest Panel Judges: These are teachers who spend countless hours thoughtfully grading each essay for creativity and uniqueness. A Contest Panel Judge is allowed only to grade essays outside of his or her own school.

Contest Winner: A student who is chosen to receive an unmounted African garnet or a Brazilian amethyst. Entrants must be creative and catch the attention of the contest panel judges.

Diamond Mom™: The mother of a Diamond Winner. The highest honor a mother can receive. On Diamond Day, Diamond Moms are given a red rose corsage to wear over their hearts.

Diamond Teacher™: The teacher of a Diamond Winner. The highest honor a teacher can receive.

Diamond Day™: The date to commemorate the Diamond Winners, their Diamond Moms, and their Diamond Teachers. The first Diamond Day in 1993 was held on Mother's Day.

Diamond Winner™: The grand prize student who is chosen to receive a quarter-carat diamond to give to mom. A Diamond Winner holds the highest honor of the contest and receives this most precious of gems to give to mom.

FlyUp!®: Acronym for Fully Live Your Unlimited Potential. The motivational and educational program developed to inspire children and adults to take chances and never give up on their dreams. Logo designed by Sean Wright.

Moon Over Mountains®: From the acronym MOM, the registered trademark is a symbol designed to remind a mother of her child. While experimenting with the word mom, I realized that the letter M resembled mountains. When the circular O was placed above the M, it looked like a moon. The word "mom" appeared miraculously. This eventually became a jewelry line for mothers. "The moon is always expressing something deep, calm, and tender, like the love of a mother for her child." -Thich Nhat Hahn. Now whenever we gaze at the moon, especially as it peeks above the mountains, we will think of our mothers.

Raise Your Balloon™: To promote the appreciation for all mothers, the company releases biodegradible balloons filled with pink carnation seeds.

Raise Your Umbrella™: The first motivational program brought into the school system to inspire kids to express themselves with confidence. Logo designed by Sean Wright.

The Legendary Contest®: This is a registered trademark and has the same meaning as the Why Mom Deserves a Diamond contest. This is defined as a "writing contest in which kids can honor their mothers and have the chance to win a diamond or gemstone."

Why Mom Deserves a Diamond®: The current style of logo used today first appeared on the 2000 anthology book of winners called, A Millennium Mother's Day Tribute. Logo designed by Michael Lynch.

# Bibliography


American Adoption Congress. www.americanadoptioncongress.org.

Berger, Peter L. An Invitation to Sociology. – A Humanistic Perspective. Pelican. 1966.

Biography.com, Anna Jarvis- Mother of Modern Mother's Day. May 12, 2012.

Bounds, Gwendolyn, How Handwriting Trains the Brain- Forming Letters Is Key to Learning, Memory, Ideas. Wall Street Journal. Oct. 5, 2010.

Jean, Dorothy. May 1, 1997. Jeweler Awards Gem in Why Mom Deserves a Diamond contest. Costa Mesa Breeze.

Hanh, Thich Nhat. Essential Writings. Orbis Books. 2001.

——. Living Buddha. Living Christ. 1995. Riverhead Books.

Huntington Beach/ Fountain Valley Independent. May, 1993. Mom is a Gem, and so is a Poem.

indifferentlanguages.com/words/mother

Josh Mapes May 12, 2012. Story of Anna Jarvis. Anna Jarvis: Mother of Modern Mother's Day. http://www.mothersdaycelebration.com/story-of-anna-jarvis.html.

Los Angeles Times. Newport jeweler's contest honors moms as reflection of his life's journey. Hannah Fry. January 2, 2015.

Loyd, Sam. Cyclopedia of Puzzles. The Lamb Publishing Company, 1914.

Maslow, Abraham. A Theory of Human Motivation (originally published in Psychological Review, 1943, Vol. 50 #4, pp. 370–396).

Maslow, Abraham, Motivation and Personality (1st edition: 1954, 2nd edition: 1970, 3rd edition 1987.)

NY Daily News. States fight to keep cursive handwriting in the classroom. Associated Press. November 15, 2013.

Pfister, Marcus. Milo and the Magical Stones. NorthSouth. Reissue edition January 1, 2010.

Watson, Michael C. Why Mom Deserves A Diamond® Anthology Books. Gallery of Diamonds Publishing. Costa Mesa, CA. 1993-2012.

——. Moon Over Mountains – The Search for Mom. Moon Over Mountains Publishing. Santa Ana, CA. 2016.

——. Adopted Like Me – Chosen to Search for Truth, Identity, and a Birthmother. Gallery of Diamonds Publishing. Costa Mesa, CA. 2005.

——. In Search of Mom. Gallery of Diamonds Publishing. Costa Mesa, CA. 1998.

# Index

**A**

Abbas, Farzana  96, 114
Abbas, Neha  96, 114
achievement  23, 125, 126
Addison, TX  73
adopted  9, 19, 33
Adopted Like Me  3, 131
affection  35, 36, 125
Afzali, Guita  102, 109
Amarillo, TX  76
Ambuehl Elementary  90
amethyst  129
Anaheim, CA  85, 94
anthology  23, 25, 32, 34
Apple Valley, CA  75
archive  51, 52, 54, 55, 57
Arroyo Seco Junior High  71
Avis, Ra  8, 11, 62, 63, 110, 111, 114

**B**

Banifatemi, Kevin  86
Banifatemi, Mojdeh  86
Barber, Cristina  112
Barraco, Dianne  70
Barraco, Jessica  70
Bathgate Elementary  80
Becker Middle School  87
Belton, MO  81
Benson Elementary  94
Bernardo Yorba Middle  70
Bethel Baptist School  91
Binford Elementary  73
biological family  31, 118
birthmother  13, 20, 21
Blood, Kathy  108
Blood, Nancy  71
Blood, Vicki Ann  71, 108
Bloomington, IN  73
Bond, Alyssa  90
Bond, Cheryl  90
Brea, CA  84
Brookhaven Elementary  88

Bruner, Michael  110, 111
Buena Park, CA  76
Buffalo, NY  77
Butterfield, Gage  62, 94, 120
Buttle, Jodi  83
Buttle, Tyler  83

**C**

California Virtual Academy  97
Candelaria, Ryan  62, 110, 111
Canyon View Elementary  91
Capistrano Valley High  67, 88
carnation  30, 34, 127, 128, 130
Cataldi, Laura  77
Cataldi, Pauline  77
Chae, Laura  87
Chae, Sue  87
Chippewa Middle School  78
Choi, Sera  87
Choi, Mi Keong  87
Christian, Jo  106
Cisneros, Ernesto  63
Cluttey, Carole  82
Cluttey, Logan  82
Colorado Springs, CO  85
Common Core  7, 34
confidence  23, 34, 121, 122, 125, 130
Connella, Alyssa  79
Connella, Michele  79
Contest Panel Judge  32, 44, 53, 112, 129
Contest Winner  129
Cordillera Elementary  69
Corona del Mar, CA  68
corporation  29
Costa Mesa  22, 31, 131
Costa Mesa Breeze  22, 131
Courreges Elementary  95
Crescent Intermediate  94
Croft, Lindsey  84
Croft, Lynne  84
Cunningham, Andrew  113
Cunningham, Dean  113

Cunningham, Karen  113
Cunningham, Matthew  113
curriculum  118
cursive  40, 42, 131
Cyclopedia of Puzzles  118, 131
Cypress, CA  97

**D**

Darakjian, Diane  69, 107
Darakjian, Megan  69, 107
Debowski, E.J.  80
Debowski, Lisa  80
Delphos, OH  78
De Marco, Debbra  63
De Portola Elementary  83, 86
Diamond Day  129
Diamond Winner  13, 21, 31, 129
Dr. Seuss  117
Duplissey, David  37, 90
Duplissey, Deanne  37, 90
Dziad, Denise  82
Dziad, Travis  82

**E**

Eastshore Elementary  70
Edison High School  22, 66
Eller, Jennifer  94
Enriquez, Mery  75
Enriquez, Sandy  75

**F**

Fairmont Private School  93
figurative language  7, 34
Fill, Lorraine  102, 109
Flickinger, Marina  111
FlyUp  6, 34, 122, 123, 124, 125, 126, 130
Fountain Valley, CA  89, 95, 131
franchise  29, 33
Fred Moiola  89
Fully Live Your Unlimited Potential  123, 126, 130

**G**

Gallegos, Lucero  63, 98
Gallery of Diamonds  13, 19, 27, 29, 31, 32, 33, 34, 35, 39, 44, 99, 104, 105, 110, 111, 115, 118, 126, 131
Garden Grove, CA  75
garnet  23, 129
gemstones  24, 27, 32, 43, 49
Gilbert Elementary  75
Glidden, Gerlyn  88
Glidden, Michael  88
gold  33, 34, 70, 73, 75, 88, 89
Goodell, Cheryl  78
Grand Opening  50
Grass Valley, CA  84
Greenville, SC  82
Groton, Analyse  86
Groton, Patricia  86
Guatemalan girl  118

**H**

Haggerty, Erica  84
Haggerty, Judith  84
handwriting  41, 131
Harbor Day School  68
Hargas, Ruby  62
Hearn, Wendy  90
Heartland High School  81
Hernandez, Carmen  79
Hernandez, Jr., Jesus  79
Holiday Spirit of the Year  31
Hong, Xu  110
Houston, TX  79
Hudson, Harry  80
Hudson, Mahgabien  80
Huntington Beach, CA  66, 131
Huynh, Kimberly  89
Huynh, Linda  89

**I**

imagination  20, 41, 123
Indianapolis courthouse  118
In Search of Mom  3, 32, 131

Irvine, CA  69, 70, 72, 87, 91, 92, 93, 95
Irvine High School  69

## J

Jarvis, Anna Marie  127
Jarvis, Anna Reeves  127
Jean, Dorothy  22, 131
Jeweler  22, 131
Jim Thorpe Fundamental  89
John Malcolm Elementary  80
John O. Tynes  96

## K

Kaufman, Deanna  93
Kaufman, Makenzie  93
keepsake  14
Ketchersid, Margaret  13, 21, 66
Ketchersid, Ruth  66
Kiang, Kathleen  68, 107
Kiang, Lauren  68, 107
Kim, Gina  36, 63, 97
Kim, Michelle  74
Kim, Paula  74
Kim, Sue  36, 63, 97, 109
Kircher, Scott  68
Kircher, Valerie  68
Kirstein, Heather  72, 108
Kirstein, Jason  72, 108
Korenberg, Leah  92, 110
Korenberg, Stephanie  92, 110
Kreidler, Ashley  78
Kreidler, Mary Jo  78

## L

La Frossia, Veronica  112
Laguna Niguel, CA  80
Lakewood, CA  71
Lamanski, Pauline  76
Lamanski, Tiffany  76
Lanham Act  32
La Palma, CA  92
La Paz Intermediate  68, 79

Las Vegas, NV  87
Lee, Lauren  37, 93
Lee, Michelle  37, 93
Legendary Contest  3, 33
Leo Carrillo Elementary  113
Linda Vista Elementary  86
Lin, Xin  96
Loi, Thomas  91
Long, Christian  115
Los Alamitos, CA  90, 91
Los Alisos Intermediate  74, 81
Los Angeles  26
Los Angeles, CA  26, 72, 108, 131
Los Coyotes Elementary  92
love  8, 12, 20, 21, 27, 30, 35, 36, 37, 38, 43, 44, 51, 54, 55, 57, 66, 68, 69, 70, 71, 73, 77, 79, 81, 83, 85, 86, 87, 88, 122, 126, 130
Loyd, Sam  118

## M

MacArthur Fundamental  96, 125
Magers, Emily  85
Magers, Kyong  85
Margaret Landell Elementary  97
Maslow, Abraham  131
master database  32
Master Diamond Cutter  54
McGinnis, Amanda  102, 109
Mendez Fundamental  98
Milo and the Magical Stones  47, 131
Mission Viejo, CA  67, 68, 69, 74, 79, 80, 81, 83, 86, 88
Moon Over Mountains  3, 33, 131
Moore, De'Anna  94
Mosher, Gavin  97
Mosher, Sheryl  97
Mother's Day  3, 13, 22, 23, 127, 128, 129, 131
Murphy, Alison  67
Murphy, Sandy  67

## N

Nardin Academy  77

Nevada Union High  84
New Albany, IN  31, 77
Newport Beach  29, 33
Nguyen, Stephen  110, 111
Northcutt Elementary  112

**O**

Oak Middle School  90
Ogles, Terry  106
Okemos, MI  78
Olivares, Danali  63, 98
Olsen-Phillips, Chris  73
Olsen-Phillips, Deb  73
Orange, CA  25, 26, 29, 31, 32, 34, 51,
        74, 86
Orange County  25, 26, 29, 31, 32, 34,
        51
Orange County Public Library  25
Orange County Register  31

**P**

Penner, Grace  88
Penner, Laura  88
Peraza, Vince  110, 111
Perkins, Blair  74
Perkins, Wendi  74
Perone, Janey  102, 109, 110, 111
Pham, Benjamin  95
Pham, Chuong  106
Pham, Yuung  95, 109
Placentia, CA  88, 96
Plankenhorn, Janet  71, 108
Plankenhorn, Jennifer  71, 108
pride  34, 39, 44, 121
prize  13, 21, 22, 24, 36, 43, 45, 129
Punzalan, Jason  85
Punzalan, Lucrecia  85

**R**

Raise Your Balloon  34
Raise Your Umbrella  34, 122, 124, 126
Rancho San Joaquin Middle  92
Rancho Santa Margarita, CA  82

Ravy, Nancy  70, 108
Ravy, Tawnya  70, 108
religion  54
Reyes, Luis  63, 114
robbery  32
Rodriguez, Jeanette  62, 102, 109, 110,
        111
Ruig, Valarie  112
Ruiz, Margarite  72
Ruiz, Roberto  72

**S**

San Juan Capistrano, CA  90
Santa Ana, CA  4, 30, 34, 89, 93, 96,
        98, 115, 124, 125, 131
sapphires  24, 75, 80
Scarsciotti, Tina  94
Scarsciotti, Tony  62, 94
Scott, Kathy  81
Scott, Matthew  81
Scruggs, Jennifer  76
Scruggs, Laura  76
self-assurance  121
self-esteem  7, 23, 34, 39, 44, 118, 121,
        125
self-worth  44
Servite High School  85
Sierra Vista Middle School  87
silver  33, 90
Simsarian, Anne Marie  83
Simsarian, Aris  83
Sintora, Fernando  63
Sipkovich, Marsha  112
Sleepy Hollow Elementary  76
Slunka, Genevieve  69
Slunka, Sherry  69
social values  51
St. Angela Merici  84
Stephen Nguyen  110, 111
stepping beyond yourself
    stepping beyond oneself  6, 117
Stern, Sarah  95
St. Johns  78
St. Malachy  72
St. Mary's  82
St. Pancratius  71

St. Pius V  76
St. Thomas High School  79
St. Timothy Episcopal  75

**T**

Taft Elementary  74
Taylor, Lisa  77
Taylor, Victor  77
Thai, Jennifer  91
Timberview Middle School  85
Tomberlin, Cathy  75
Tomberlin, Rachel  75
Tomlinson, Brice  73
Tomlinson, Jackie  73
Trabuco Canyon, CA  97
trademark  32, 33, 129, 130
trade secrets  29
Trinity Christian Academy  73
Tustin, CA  94
Tweedie, Matthew  63, 114

**U**

umbrella  34, 109, 121
US Patent and Trademark  33
University High  95

**V**

Valencia, CA  71
Vazquez, Luz  89
Vazquez, Sophia  89
Vista Verde  93

**W**

Waldman, Hara  95
Watson, Carmen  8, 11, 22, 31, 62, 63,
        102, 103, 105, 106, 108, 109,
        110, 111, 114, 118
Watson, Martha  4, 8, 18, 33, 107
Watson, Michaela  8, 62, 63, 111, 114
Watson, Patricia  8
Westwood Basics Plus  72
Wheeler, Amanda  81

Wheeler, Kelly  81
Why Mom Deserves a Diamond  1, 6,
        10, 11, 14, 19, 21, 22, 23, 28,
        29, 32, 33, 35, 39, 48, 51, 101,
        104, 125, 126, 130, 131
Wilson Elementary  124
words (positive, power of, spoken)  7,
        8, 14, 19, 21, 22, 26, 36, 37,
        39, 41, 43, 44, 45, 50, 51, 52,
        54, 55, 57, 71, 92, 99, 117, 122,
        123, 128, 131
Wright, Patricia  111
Wright, Sean  110, 111
writing contest  19, 103, 118, 130

**X**

Xu, Charlie  92
Xu, Hong  92

**Y**

Yorba Linda, CA  70
Young, Nikki  96

**Z**

Zhong, Xin  91
Zhou, Harvey  91

Made in the USA
Monee, IL
07 July 2026

56553278R00075